VOODOO NATION

A Personal Narrative by Martyn Jones

ISBN: 978-1-9163097-1-5

Copyright 2020

i2i Publishing. Manchester.

www.i2ipublishing.co.uk

To my Grandsons James, Will and Samet
who insisted I write this narrative.

Contents

Prologue

The Whispering Voice

Was the whispering voice speaking to me? I asked myself as I lifted my head from the pillow, confused and wondering if I was dreaming. The voice continued to whisper in the same toneless, calm way, as it had reached gently into my sleep, slowly bringing me to consciousness and now awareness.

"He has a gun at my head. He is going to shoot. I need help now."

I frowned, trying to understand what was happening.

"I am at the Iron Bridge, the bottom of Ibo Lele hill. I need someone here now."

The voice spoke with no sense of urgency, and I continued to wonder at the eerie calmness of this surreal voice in my head, re-enforcing the thought in my sleep fogged mind, *I must be dreaming*, as once more, the whispering voice calmly began to repeat its message.

"He has a gun to my head. He's going to shoot......."

Now the realisation dawned in my befuddled brain, the voice was not coming from inside my head. I was not dreaming. The voice was coming from behind my head. I rolled over and in the pale darkness of my room, I realised that the voice was coming from my personal radio on the bedside table.

I sat up, taking the radio in my hand, gazing with curious interest and puzzlement at the instrument, while the voice continued its disquieting message.

The penny dropped!

I double clicked the radio send button, telling the voice I had received the message. I exploded from the bed, switched on the bedside table lamp and reached for my clothing and all my immediate action gear which I would lay out at night on the spare bed knowing I would otherwise be groping and stumbling around looking for it, should there be a night alarm.

Less than two minutes later, still struggling into my tac vest, I reached under my pillow, palmed my Glock pistol and stuffed it into the vest's holster. I would put up with the odd oil stain on the sheets for knowing, at night, in the dark, it was at my fingertips. There was always something menacing about the night in Haiti.

I grabbed the M16 rifle from the bed, the radio from the bedside table and moved quickly to the door, there forcing myself to stop, wait and listen before cautiously opening the door, making sure there was nothing nasty lurking in the darkness. I stepped through the door just as Chris came crashing from his room still struggling into his tac vest and trying not to drop his Uzi sub machine gun.

"You heard it too, Chris?"

"Yeah. Who is it?"

We both raced through the once renowned hotel where decades previously, it had been the hedonistic playground of the French traveller before this beautiful island paradise of Haiti was turned into a neglected, murderous and brutal dictatorship by

Papa Doc and later, Baby Doc Duvalier. Now the Ibo Lele had long since been allowed to fade away into an almost fairy tale sleep. No tourists came to Haiti now, apart from the curious, the missionaries, those fleeing justice, and of course, the likes of Ed, Chris and me. The Ibo Lele was tired, faded and careworn, echoing Haiti itself.

Apart from the gardens….

We ran through the arched garden walkway, unlike the hotel, still neatly kept, as if a garden spirit, perhaps Flora herself, tended the gardens, while the building continued its long decaying sleep. Then again, this is a Voodoo nation Chris and I were working in. So perhaps it was Erzulie, the Voodoo spirit of flowers, pleasure and all things sweet?

It then came to me, the whispering voice was Juan, a former US Navy Seal who delighted in telling us, all he wanted to do was sit on a tropical beach, any tropical beach, anywhere. So of course, his radio call sign was 'Beach'.

"Juan, it's Juan," I gasped.

We were both breathless as we reached the big four-wheel drive. Others may or may not have heard Juan's message, they would get there or not, but our pal Juan needed help now. I climbed behind the wheel and started the vehicle. Chris threw himself onto the passenger seat as I rammed the stick into drive and roared away from the hotel. I knew Juan's location was only a couple of minutes away but did not know how long he had had a gun to his head. I drove recklessly down the hill, then checked myself, *best to get there a few seconds late than not get there at all,* I reasoned, as I tasted the familiar saltiness on my lips. My nose was bleeding. It always did briefly, as my pulse rate and blood pressure soared with fear and expectation, as my body supercharged itself for whatever was about to happen.

There were no words between Chris and I during that brief and very rapid drive to the Iron Bridge, each of us in our own lonely place, our thoughts wondering fearfully as to what was waiting for us just a few seconds away now.

The Iron Bridge made its usual grating, grumbling protest as our vehicle crossed it and we immediately saw three Haitian national police officers standing by Juan's car. One had a rifle pointed through the driver's window at Juan's head, and the two others standing together next to the first, both with pistols in their hands.

I skidded the vehicle to a stop, feet from the policemen. Chris was first out, leaving his Uzi on the seat, and walking towards the police, his hands raised, a smile on his face, he repeated over and over "Packy problem," Haitian patois for "No problem," as I slipped from the vehicle, armed the M16, flicked on 'full auto' and aimed at the three police officers.

No doubt of my intentions. It was now down to them, either they lived or died as now, their pistols were levelled at Chris.

Chris, a former Avon and Somerset police officer and my friend, was playing a very courageous and dangerous game. I had no intention of losing him to these three rogue police officers. The racking, or arming, of a weapon has a distinctive sound, instantly recognised, never forgotten, and never mistaken for anything else, immediately getting people's attention. They had moments to live.

There is no street lighting in Port au Prince, it was dark, only the pale noon light and both vehicles' head lights giving any illumination to this increasingly atmospheric scene, re-enforcing the thought that someone was going to die here very shortly. I shook these thoughts from my mind, clearing my head as I prepared myself to take three lives, and heard the still whispering voice of Juan, now with an undertone of urgency.

"He's going to shoot. You must do something now! He's going to shoot."

Don't lose it now, Juan. I remember thinking.

I instinctively knew the policeman with the rifle meant to kill. I recognised it in the casual slack expression on his face. I saw it in his emotionless eyes, read it in his body language. He would show no mercy, he had no mercy, he had come to rob and kill, and I shuddered inwardly with the same primal fear that an animal must feel when faced with a predator. My very soul told me it was so, and I knew I was going to kill him first.

The other two looked quizzically from Chris to me, unsure now, uncertainty now dawning on them. One, I knew, was also a killer who had and would use his powerful and mostly unaccountable position as a Haitian police officer to rob, rape and kill. His much younger companion, obviously still a rookie, was just learning the perks of his office from the two much older, experienced, cynical and murderous comrades.

"How old is he?" The thought flashed through my head, *"seventeen, maybe eighteen?"* He had a fresh, youthful, open face, and I saw fear in his eyes.

Chris was speaking softly to the three Haitian officers, trying to make them understand in the local patois, trying to hold their attention. I heard Juan repeating over Chris' appeal, still in the same almost detached matter-of-fact whispering voice, "He's going to shoot me, do something."

Chris turned and looked appealingly at me and said quietly, with a note of resignation "This is going to rat shit. Over." And stepped aside.

"Drop Chris!" I said softly and began to squeeze the trigger……

How did I ever get to this point in my life?

Well, it had been a long and sometimes bumpy road. Let me start somewhere near the beginning……

Chapter 1

Road to Kennyland's Park

I remember being taken to nursery daily by my mum. She was working at the time in a factory, and she needed to get there on time. Only this morning, she had misunderstood me. I had wanted, no needed her, to kiss me goodbye that morning. She had just delivered me to one of the uniformed nurses and turned to hurry away to catch her bus. I must have cried out desperate to have her kiss, she turned towards me, but the uniformed nursery nurse told her to get on. Mum turned and hurried off, calling she would collect me at four o'clock.

I broke down in floods of tears, totally and profoundly inconsolable the rest of the day, and that presumably minor incident, one of my earliest memories, has stayed with me throughout my life. Of course, back then in the forties, just a couple or so years after World War Two had ended, civilians like my mum, automatically obeyed those in uniform. I remember outside the cinemas, or *"The pictures,"* as we would call them, big tall men, dressed in military style greatcoats and peaked caps holding sway over the dozens eagerly and compliantly waiting in queues for the next performance. No one ever bucked their authority, and of course, doctors, nurses and well everyone in any type of authority, must have had training in 'No nonsense attitude.' But this seemingly unimportant event at a nursery left this little boy devastated.

I remember one Guy Fawkes night; I must have been recovering from a childhood illness. I was made to sit at the French windows in an armchair, in the warm and watch my mum, my aunts, uncles and cousins outside in the garden enjoying the fireworks party. I felt very left out. Every now and then, one of my uncles would come up to the French windows and put a firework just outside and I would dive behind the armchair covering my head, expecting the windows to be blown in as they had been during the bombing. Land mines floating down attached to parachutes bringing silent death and destruction, the Doodlebugs, and later the V2s. There was a family story that on hearing a Doodlebug's engine cut out somewhere in the sky above our house, my grandfather picked me up and threw me down the cellar stairs. Doodlebugs killed masses of civilians and reeked huge amounts of damage, one hitting a cinema not far from our house, killing dozens of children watching cartoons.

I remember also I had become aware of the term bastard. I am a product of a wartime liaison; my mum had been in the Women's Royal Army Corps from the beginning of the war, and during the blitz had driven lorries filled with ammunition delivering the ordinance to Ack Ack sites. Later, she had become a Colonel's driver and was mentioned in dispatches. Mum had been married and divorced, had met my father, and I was the issue. My grandfather had ordered my father out of the house when I was a babe-in-arms. *"Owt of the howse!"* It was never spoken of again. Except for years later in my early teens, I was told by an older cousin who had witnessed this small family drama, my father had left with tears in his eyes.

He had loved me.

Much later, when I was in my thirties, an aunt asked if I would want to trace my father. I thought before answering and remember thinking that if he had wanted to trace me, I would not be hard to find, and left it at that. He, of course, had moved on with his life, and who would blame him? In those days, being ordered to leave by a head of a family was final and heavy stuff. But then again, I have always wondered. I like to think that sometimes, he would have thought about me, as I have always wondered about him. Sometimes, when mum and I were on the bus returning home from shopping, we would pass a full-sized billboard just a short distance from our bus stop and there, on the upper half of this huge board, was the picture of a Guardsman in a red tunic and bearskin. He was a good-looking man with a neatly trimmed moustache and knowing eyes, and mum would whisper to me, "That's your dad." As I recall, it was a cigarette advert.

So, I was born to a single mother, a divorced woman, who in those days, some seventy years ago, would have been very much outside excepted social norms. I heard the term bastard used referring to me at times, not understanding the term, but leaving me unsettled and confused. It must be said that a section of my family always left me with the feeling of not quite belonging. I still have that sense of exclusion today with those that are still here.

I remember though, I had a happy childhood, and those who loved me made that abundantly clear. In those days, even as young school kids, me and my mates would wander quite some distance from home, playing, climbing trees and getting into all kinds of scrapes. I think now, that even then, I was looking for adventure.

Bird nesting was the sport of early summer, and I would climb trees, tunnel into hedges looking for bird nests. One time, I had climbed a huge cedar to reach a nest. The knack was to get down with the eggs intact. You could not put them in your pocket as they would likely be crushed. So, the trick was to put them into your mouth to carry them down. This time, however, I slipped, and then quickly regained my hold on the branch, but in my alarm had bitten down on the eggs filling my mouth with slime. Ugh!

Happy days.

Mum and I lost our home, 53 Kingswood Road, when I was about nine years old. I have no idea of the circumstances, something about my grandparents having to surrender the lease. The bailiff arrived one morning with a police officer and ordered us out of the house. I remember walking away from our home, mum pushing her bike with a suitcase full of our clothing, resting on the handlebars, and me walking besides her and seeing neighbours spying on us through their lace curtains, their interest stirred by the policeman and the official looking man in a suit and tie, carrying a briefcase. Looking back at that day now brings tears to my eyes. Mum would never speak of it, nor would name those who had brought us to this predicament.

We walked to the shops, the shops we called 'Up the top', and mum began looking in shop windows at the postcards, looking for lodgings for the night. I do not recall any of our family about on that day. Mum must have found a post card advertising a lodging house nearby and we walked from the shops to the house, as I recall, about twenty minutes away.

She knocked on the door which was answered by a kindly lady some years older than mum. We were told there was no room, but she invited us in for a cup of tea. I remember we spent two nights there, this dear lady allowed us to sleep in her front room, she even made up a bed for me. The following day, mum went cap in hand to the family, and I was taken in by my auntie Ann. Mum got nurse's accommodation in the hospital, she was working as a healthcare assistant, known then as an auxiliary nurse. There she stayed for something over two years, and I stayed with my auntie, uncle and cousin Neil. Every Friday after work, mum would go to the Town Hall housing department and repeat her request for a council flat. There was a council waiting list, and it took those years before she was finally given one. At that time, her repeated visits to the housing department gave credits to her application for council housing.

By that time, I was in boarding school which somewhat eased the pressure on mum, and on school holidays, I would be put up in whatever lodgings mum was in at the time. She later told me that she could no longer stay in the soulless hospital accommodation. When not on duty, mum would have to sit in her room. Luckily, she was a reader, and she loved the Agatha Christie books which were all the rage at the time. Her room was illuminated by one naked bulb hanging by a dusty wire from the ceiling, giving a cold stark light, and she had promised herself that one day when she got her flat, the first piece of furniture she would buy would be a chandelier. And she did. I arrived back from school on holiday and she took me home to our new council flat, and there was the chandelier hanging in our front room. Then she told me the story of her room in the hospital.

We had a home again, together again and everything was going to be alright.

I have never forgotten that dear lady taking mum and me into her house for those couple of nights. In my mind, I have always thanked her. As I recall, the house was in Aldborough Road, just a couple of streets down from Kingswood Road.

I had just turned eleven when mum had sent me to boarding school. She had been awarded a grant from the Ilford County Council. I was fearful of going to this strange place and terrified of being separated from mum again, as the school was in Oxfordshire, and to me, hundreds of miles from mum. But remember, I was living with an aunt, and mum was living, well sleeping and reading Agatha Christie in her Spartan nurse's accommodation, working mostly nights.

It was years later; I came to realise that mum sending me to Kennylands was the greatest gift she could ever have given me. I blossomed there.

Kennylands Park School

I had just turned 11-years old when mum gave my suitcase to the driver and saw me onto the coach. I dare not kiss her goodbye nor be kissed, I was now all grown up. But I remember desperately wanting to, but too embarrassed to, in front of the other boys and girls. Yes, it was a mixed boarding school. A master showed me to my seat and introduced me to a tearful boy in the next seat and told me my new friend would look after me. I can still see this boy's face but cannot recall his name. The first thing he said to me was, "I'm homesick" and began sobbing.

Weeks before, mum and I had been interviewed by the headmaster of Kennylands at the Ilford Town Hall. He had a stern, wrinkled, grim and heavily jowled face. He asked what I would do if I did not like living at Kennylands.

Being just 11-years old and of course, quite guileless, I answered honestly that I would get on the first bus and go home. Of course, mum jumped in, saying I would write to her first and she would of then discuss me "with you, headmaster." This man turned and looked at me with suspicious eyes and said nothing. Throughout my years at Kennylands, his expression never changed when looking at, or speaking to me.

The following morning after a night spent quietly crying into my pillow, and following breakfast in the dining hall, and morning assembly, I was summoned to the headmaster's office. There, this man sat behind a large desk with the same expression I remembered from a few weeks previously. I was not invited to sit and stood nervously to attention under his suspicious gaze. He then gave me a severe dressing down, warning me that he would be keeping his eye on me. He then ordered me out of the office. I had thought, silly boy, that I was to be welcomed to the school.

11 years old! First day in a strange place! Away from home! What was this man thinking of? He had obviously taken a degree in 'No nonsense attitude' and graduated with honours.

A couple of years later, he stopped me as I was walking to class and asked, with that same, grim, jowled face and suspicious eyes, "Why is your mother's surname different to yours?" I mumbled something to the effect that mum was divorced and most of all, I remember thinking, *He knows I'm a bastard now!*

Disgusting man, I would never forgive him.

But, despite that first day, and the headmaster, over the next few weeks and months, I first blossomed and then bloomed into boarding school life and became, over the following years a decent sportsman and proved to myself and my long despairing teachers that I wasn't as thick witted as perhaps they, and certainly I, had thought.

I remember in my first term, I had discovered I could run, run fast. Never a distance runner but anything up to 400 metres, or in pounds, shillings and pence, 440 yards, I would be a contender, and that first summer, I learnt to high jump. The 'Scissors' method was still being taught for the high jump, but I was shown the 'Western Roll', a new high jump technique from America, which I took to immediately. But I think my most successful field event was the 'hop, skip, and jump,' known today as the triple jump. The peak of my school athletic career was in my last year at Kennylands, representing Oxfordshire in the 1957 All England Schools Championships at Houlton Le Spring, Durham. It was cold up north, and I had had my tracksuit bottoms stolen in the triple jump waiting area and had got cold waiting for my jumps. I finished with a bronze medal. I could have been a champion if not for my stolen tracksuit bottoms! Or so I keep telling myself.

So, I could run fast and had started to play football. But it must be said, NOT VERY WELL! The problem that I am left-handed and therefore, left footed, and could only kick with some degree of accuracy, and accuracy isn't really the right word, with my left foot. So, as a sprinter and only left footed, I became the dashing left winger in the school team.

I would sprint and outrun the other team down the left wing and cross the ball with occasional accuracy to my forwards waiting in anticipation, their fingers crossed. But mostly, I dumped the ball at the other team's feet.

I was never allowed to take a corner kick, and the standing joke among my teammates was that instead of aiming at the goal, I would aim at the chicken huts way off in the other direction. Believe me when I say I was only in the school football team because I could run very fast with the ball under control, some of the time.

Now cricket, that is a game I really enjoyed and became a moderately decent bowler and batsman in the school team.

I remember the serious stuff too: Lessons. At first, I really struggled, but for the patience of Mrs Downer and others. French, well Mr Dewandeler, or Dickie, as he was not too affectionately called, just gave up on me, although out of necessity, much later, found I could pick it up quickly. Maths, apart from simple adding and subtracting, was just Chinese to me. The subjects I really took a liking to and moderately successful at were, English and English composition, perhaps because I was a reader like mum, and history and geography.

Subjects such as the sciences etc., were not taught in Secondary Modern schools at that time. Another subject we all had endure was religious studies, not the all-embracing philosophical subject it is today, but then it was learning and reading the bible; boring stuff for young schoolboys and girls. However, one of these lessons is still etched in my memory. The Headmaster took this subject on that day, and we had two Jewish youngsters in the class, Ruth and David, I can remember David's surname but not Ruth's, I'm sorry Ruth. As the headmaster entered the classroom, he said forcefully to Ruth and David, using their surnames, "Get out!" So, I was not the only one he was nasty to I thought, re-enforcing my dislike for this man.

I remember that over the 4 years or so I was at Kennylands, there were some of the happiest days of my life as I grew from boyhood into a young man. Warm summer afternoons meeting girls in the school field, especially at the weekends, chatting to them and listening to cricket on the new-fangled radios that worked from batteries. What were they called? Every Saturday evening, we had the school dance where us boys got to dance with the girls. Marion you were a lovely dancer, I hope your toes have recovered. Freezing winters sometimes meant having 6 blankets on my bed. We had heating in the dormitories but the fire buckets next to my bed still froze solid every night.

And then, as suddenly, as it had all started, my schooldays were over, and I was now to find my way in the big wide world.

.

Chapter 2

Early 'Doors'

I remember leaving school and feeling like a fish out of water for some months. My school days were spent in boarding school and my school mates were now scattered all over Essex. Soon, I was to lose touch with most of them. The first few jobs I had were just boring and I was fired often for rudeness to my superiors who spent most of the time looking down their noses at the likes of me. Of course, the problem was that my head was filled with ripping yarns from the copious amounts of adventure books I had read at school, leaving me being unable to settle. Everything about my life at that time was BORING. I needed stimulus, adventure, only I did not know what or where to find it.

I had an older cousin, some ten years older than I, who was a body builder and went to a gym regularly throughout the week. I joined him. It was there, I was to enter a whole new world and meet characters that I had only seen in the old B-movies that I had no idea existed in real life.

Barry and Bobby took me under their wings. They both worked as bouncers or minders, as they were also known, at the back of pubs, where at night, after closing time, which was at 10.30pm in those days, would become late night unlicensed drinking houses, known as drinkers. These two were not doormen as they are known today, as night clubs and bars these days, are almost churches compared to those uncontrolled, dens of violence, vice and iniquity. The bouncers were not employed to keep out undesirables, no, if these people or anyone else, had cash in their pockets, they were welcome, until they had spent it all. Anti-social behaviour, as it is termed today, was tolerated until the fighting started as that, of course, interrupted others from spending at the bar. So then, the bouncers or bouncer, usually just one tough, rough, brute of a man, would step in and beat the daylights out of the offenders, allowing everyone else to continue their drinking. No-one ever barred these violent and sadistic characters; they would have had to burn the place down for the management to even consider baring anyone. Anyone injured, either from the beatings, glassing, stabbings or razors, would be carried around the corner and up the road to keep this bad publicity and any police investigation, away from the drinker.

Barry and Bobby were not nice people, but they both took a liking to me and invited me into their world. I could not tell mum what I was up to, and without her guiding hand, I took this wrong turning in life, not my first mistake, although one which since then, has dictated how my life has turned out. Looking back, it was the wrong path; I had turned left instead of right. It's all too easy to say I did not have a father to show me the right path. I had planned to join the army when old enough, but that time was still over two years away.

And so, it was in the back streets of Barking and in Ilford, I began to work with these two thugs. It became a painful introduction into a life with all the violence and other stuff that was completely alien to me, and one I knew I needed to get out of. Throughout those years I had a sense of detachment, it was not me. But then again, I was not yet 16 years old.

Bad Move

Two years on, I was eighteen years old and by now, had a reputation as a tough doorman. Door work then was a brutal late-night occupation and depending where your door was determined how much you were paid. Then the skills required were not knowledge of licensing law and the lawful managing awkward people but being able to "look after yourself" in any given violent situation. My years under the tutorage of Bobby and Barry was taking me firmly down the wrong path.

A friend from the doors, Ronnie Hall met me one afternoon and took me to see his boss Barre' Foster who was then the general manager of *The Palais*, one of the many branches of Mecca Dancing, then a top and respectable entertainment company in the sixties and seventies. Each branch was then called either a Dance Hall or Ballroom, not the generic Night Club as they are known these days. The Palais had a capacity of two thousand. It was smart, clean and the music and entertainment was supplied by the Phil Tate Orchestra a well know and popular radio dance band. Records then were only played when the band had their break. Mecca's larger Ballrooms in central London all had two orchestras such as the Lyceum, now returned to its original use as a theatre and the home of The Lion King. During WW11 the Lyceum became a dance hall because of all the thousands of American and Canadian servicemen stationed in the Home Counties, and Hammersmith Palais where Joe

Loss was the resident orchestra, and The Empire Leister Square.

Barre Foster must have liked what he saw and immediately offered me a job. Of course, Ronnie had told him I was more than "up for it" but I like to think he saw something else in me as well. I was employed as a box office manager, a posh title for head doorman really and it was there I met another pal who became a close friend Lee Hicks, we have lost touch now and I know he had health problems years ago. I hope you are well Lee, and still with us. He was a tough Billingsgate Market fish porter some years senior to me who would rib me about my posh title and taking me under his considerable wing teaching me the craft of people managing. The years I worked with Barre in Ilford and later when he was promoted and sent to Bristol was my turning point, and he put me on the straight and narrow, honing my skills in people management and running a business. I only went to Bristol in the sixties after returning from overseas because Barre had a problem with a crowd of thugs and asked me to stay for a few months and sort out the problem. I'm still here. Barre was a good man and died far too young of a heart attack.

I have forever been lucky in the people I have known and worked with, Barre changed the direction of my life, and was to become my mentor and a highly regarded family friend.

More of Barre later.

The Lion's Den

He entered the room with another. They both looked straight ahead, avoiding eye contact with everyone. They were dressed casually, and I had thought they would arrive in track suits. Steve Wride had told me that they were the Force Physical Intervention instructors. I believed they were going to be useful teaching my guys the accepted police techniques in restraint and control and looked forward to meeting them. Steve was chuffed to have them as a part of his team, training Bristol's hundreds of doormen.

I was standing with Steve as they approached. They saw only Steve, making no eye contact with me. *Alright,* I thought, they are the police and have their own corporate views on the likes of me, and the city's doormen. Okay, *stay calm and don't be offended.*

Steve Wride was a police sergeant, specialising in licensing and had been selected to organise and operate the city's training of its doormen. He was answerable to senior officers of course, but in reality, was doing all the hard work himself with what I saw as very little support from colleagues. No support, a lot of criticism of course, and sniping.

Watch your back Steve. I liked this police officer, he was a good decent man, and that shone through over the number of years we were associated.

Steve introduced me to 'them'. As I recall, we shook hands; they were painfully neutral. They then did make eye contact, but I had the impression they were observing me out of purely professional interest. *Christ!* I thought, if they believed even half the bullshit about me on the street, I was in trouble.

At the time, I was the managing director of a very successful security company that controlled a three-figure number of pub and nightclub doors. Door companies and their management were viewed very much with suspicion by the police and other authorities. However, to be able to operate a door company and not be interfered with by others wanting your doors, one needed a certain profile and associates that could be described by the word 'Muscle'! I'll come back to 'Muscle' later. It was because of this dark side of the business and the deeds one would, on occasions, have to perform, that the entire business was run from the shadows, fuelling the folk lore and overstated reputations of the characters running this very specialised and contentious type of security.

Some years later, in a very different place, the other side of the world, Chris described to me the thoughts going through his mind on that first meeting.

The diktat had come from high, meaning that senior officers had ordered them, saying: *"You will train these fucking bouncers!" Chris added that it felt like we were about to go into action having to meet Martyn Jones, and all his bouncers, and as we walked into the hall above the pub, I whispered to Jerry, "Entering the Lion's Den."*

I saw Steve Wride amongst a group of men in front of the audience and became aware of a large figure with his back to me, "I seemed to recognise its shape, "Steve said, and I noted his mischievous smile, "You know Martyn Jones, don't you?" Yes, I said instinctively. He proffered his hand to me, and I gripped it and we locked eyes as we shook hands. Did Martyn Jones hold my hand and eye lock a second longer than seemed necessary? He told me that it was not until later that he came to understand the significance of this.

Yes, I had. I did this to signal to those watching that I would be dealing with the police in future. No more of the 'never speaking to the police' nonsense. It was out of date, and with the licensing of doorman, heralded a new future in the relationship between doormen and police.

Chris went on to tell me how he described our meeting that evening: *"I knew Martyn Jones alright! He ran the biggest bouncer company in the West of England. He had not reached that kind of prominence by being a shrinking violet. His folk lore went back to the early sixties, the Krays, the East End of London. The police view was of gangsterism, rumours abounded of beatings, violent enforcement, and general unpleasantness, and was aware that Martyn Jones had been arrested for assaults but nothing for offences of dishonesty. In fact, my first encounter with him was as a green 17-year-old police cadet brazenly flashing my police warrant card to gain free admission to the Locarno way back in 1968. He would wave me through with a detached air of disdain. I had the impression that he thought "cheeky young sprog!"*

Umm.

I had been in the business since I was 15 years old. My first door was the delightful, *The Britannia Arms*, Barking in the back streets of East London. It was there and later at *The Plessey Club* in Ilford where I began to learn the craft of 'door' work. Looking back now at the experiences all these decades later, I realised I had taken the wrong turning in life. I had turned left instead of turning right and by the time I had begun to see the light, it was too late for several reasons. I had stayed too long, and of course, I made a few mistakes as you can imagine. But don't get me wrong, I have rubbed shoulders, and been associated with the very finest of people, and at the other end of the scale, the mediocre, and the very worst of them all. What had begun to get increasingly under my skin were the continual dealings with the street idiots. They were out there, continually causing problems, continually probing and testing to see if there was an opportunity they could take advantage of. That reminds me of the idiot who went into the Central Police Station in Bristol and said to the shift sergeant "If I'm beaten up, it's Martyn Jones that done it." He then proceeded to go around all my contracts in Bristol offering to take over the 'doors' for half price! This idiot's judgement had been somewhat distorted due to his misguided reliance on a steroid blotted, coke snorter of a narcissist, who spent most of the time gazing at himself in shop windows.

But I have digressed.

Constable Chris Nott and Sergeant Jerry Landor had been police officers for twenty-five years by the time of our first acquaintance, and it was obvious to me they thought we were from different worlds. To be fair to them, I carried a load of suspicious baggage, or I think they call it, antecedence. So, as I saw it, in an organisation like the police service, what outsiders or informants say to them about high profile individuals who come onto their radar screens becomes lore. It sticks and is re-enforced by all the other bullshit spoken about you.

Hey guys! I'm just like you. I have the same values and beliefs that you have for Christ's sake!

Well, to be honest, I would not tolerate any interference with my business, or my guys being attacked, or threats being issued against me personally. So, there have been occasions when I have crossed the line when dealing with those idiots, and others who have threatened me and my business. Never civilians, just those who insisted.

It was some years later, when one evening, Chris and I were having dinner in one of the fabulously decorated restaurants in Petionville, Port au Prince, Haiti, he told me the story of 'The Lion's Den.'

I had asked somewhat naively: *"Who was the Lion?"*

Chris was amused, and said: *"You were, you thug."*

I feigned surprise and thought: *"Oh to see ourselves as others do."*

At the time, we were sitting in the middle of probably the most murderous and violent, dangerous city in the northern hemisphere, and both carrying the required requisites for such a place. We were armed with a Glock pistol (there's a tragic little story about this weapon, but I'll come to that later), spare magazines, an Asp (that's a steel cosh to the uneducated) and a knife, should all else fail.

Christ, did I say that! But you get the picture.

Anyway, following their session with the doormen, I gave my presentation in what I have since been told was my usual didactic delivery style, and thinking that now, I had really confirmed their perception of me. Steve Wride bless him, said I was perfect, as I could deliver the subject at the doormen's own level. I am still wondering if there is a compliment there or not.

They left while I was speaking, saying goodbye to Steve, Chris giving me a nod, his expression wooden.

Chris was laughing that evening in Port au Prince, and to be honest, once I had gotten over the eye-opener of the Lion's Den tale, I could see the amusing side of it. From Chris and Jerry's perception, I was on the opposite side. There was a culture of not having anything to do with police, although that was beginning to change, largely due the work of officers like Steve Wride.

It was perhaps a couple of years after 'The Lion's Den' that Chris approached me one evening during the Door Safe training and told me he was retiring from the police service. Well actually, he was retiring on medical grounds. He had been involved in an accident whilst on duty that had left him with a serious neck injury. He had, by then, been a police officer for twenty-eight years, but the neck injury had resulted in it being, in his senior officer's view, unsafe for him to continue as a serving police officer.

So, what does he do with this serious neck injury? He asks me for a job.

I was hesitant, happy to grab him without a second thought, but thinking of Chris. He would have done the job easily and done it well. But, there's that but again, he would be leaving himself wide open to the inevitable disgust of former colleagues, some of them anyway. He had and still has, a few trusted friends still in the force, but, there's that 'but' again, several of his former colleagues did him a lot of damage, both to his self-esteem and his pocket when he came to work for me.

Over the years, Chris and I have worked together pretty much round the world. We have been involved in many rough houses, but one remains in my memory because of the absurdity of where it took place, and the people we were fighting. To say it was like something from an Indiana Jones movie is not an exaggeration.

We were coming out of Northern Iraq, known locally then, as Kurdistan, making our way to the nearest domestic airport in South Eastern Turkey, passing from one war zone into another, through a border post wedged between Turkey, Syria, Iran and Northern Iraq. It was the end of the world!

Zahko is a border town, where the traveller must robustly exercise caution and self-awareness. There are no prisoners taken and no second chances. Ringed by snow-capped mountains summer and winter, it is right in the middle of disputed Kurdistan. Here, mono-browed, crazed eyed Kurdish wild men would swoop down from their mountain eyrie's and attack the Turkish and Northern Iraqi security forces in the region. The whole place had a very tense atmosphere, where troops both sides of the border were very trigger happy!

Enter Chris and I....

We had passed from the Iraqi side without any problem, especially as we had a good Turkish Kurdish taxi driver who acted as a fixer and had smoothed our way through the stone faced, heavy handed officialdom.

The problems started on reaching the Turkish side of the border.

Passport Control was crowded with Turkish Kurdish tanker drivers, bringing refined petrol from Turkey to the pumps in Northern Iraq. They would have been waiting for hours, some for days, trying to return to their homes in Turkey, and of course pick up another load. They were highly paid for very dangerous work. The Taliban had begun to target them, and we were forever coming across their burnt-out tankers, and decapitated bodies on the road, and forever watching horrendous executions of these drivers on the local TV.

The Turkish passport officers were in no hurry to let them enter the country, as the way that the Turkish authorities viewed them, the Kurdish drivers were only drivers during the day and insurgents at night. We had just left one war zone and were now in the middle of another.

Many of these drivers were mono-browed, but some in that passport control room at Zahko had eyebrows that needed combing! It gave them a very wild, alien appearance. Well, they frightened me.

There were three passport officers behind the counter and every few minutes, one would climb on top of the counter and draw his pistol while the other two would come out from behind the counter, draw their batons and bash the Kurds back into a resemblance of a queue. Presumably, the Kurds did not quite understand the concept of a queue, and that was the Turkish way of dealing with that misperception. They again would stand in some sort of line for a few moments, presumably trying to understand what the Passport Control officers were on about, then again, attack the counter, shouting and waving their passports.

Chris and I had entered the room and looked questionably at our fixer. He shrugs and smiles apologetically. We were on our own! The room had turned silent, the Kurds watching us through suspicious, threatening eyes, and don't forget the mono-brows, the passport officers with their faces cold as concrete.

Right! I thought. *No point in fannying about here. Head up, plenty of swagger.* It always works, doesn't it?

I stepped up to the counter and presented my passport to a hard-faced, expressionless passport officer. Immediately, I was surrounded by a hoard of Kurds who also thrust their passports at the officer and begin shouting. The three passport officers in turn, drew their batons and begin beating the Kurds from their side of the counter. Chris and I were surrounded by this swirling mass of tribesmen. I saw a flash of a knife and thought it's about that time to start making an impression. Two Kurds reeled away from my punches, while Chris battered another behind me. Momentarily, the fighting stopped as the Kurds tried to work out what had happened, then two came back at us and were quickly put down. To be fair, they did not fight with their fists, they had their own way, with knives. No prisoners! Chris and I were unarmed.

The three passport officers ran from behind the counter, pistols drawn pointing at us. Chris and I stood open handed and smiling innocently at the officers. The senior officer beckoned us to the counter and said tersely, "Passport!" We handed over our passports and the officer stamped them, thumping the stamp down, making a loud bang on the counter, then pointed to the door ordering us both out.

Again, amused, I thought to myself; *I've been chucked out of better places than this!*

As we left the Passport Control office, the officers began beating the Kurds into a queue again with their batons.

"Right" I said, "Where's our taxi driver? Let's get out of town before that lot gets out of there!"

Chapter 3

King Street

My first introduction to King Street was in the early eighties. I had just finished managing *Tiffany's*, a night club and had taken over a security company from someone who will remain nameless, but who had had enough of the business and evacuated to sunny Spain. Where else? Spain was then a land of opportunity for the chancer. Years later, I was to come to understand how he had felt. Security is a ceaselessly tough business and takes its toll over the years. If you work on the street too long, it will get you, and I knew I must not stay too long. Too many temptations, too many dangers, too many offers you really must refuse, and sometimes to refuse would put you and your family in jeopardy. Besides, HM Revenue and Customs desperately wanted to speak to my new company's previous owner and there are still those out there who know his name. So, pre-extradition Spain for this man looked by far the best option.

At first, the street reminded me of the old westerns I would watch as a kid. It was like Dodge City when the cowboys, after hitting town, their pockets full of cash, would drink themselves senseless. In King Street, you would not walk on the pavement, as it was full of staggering, belligerent, fighting drunks. The only way to make progress on the street and not have the risk of being bloodied, was to walk in the road, or more accurately, the middle of the road. The whole place in the early eighties emitted malevolence at the weekends, and for most people, Fridays was still payday.

Unless of course you were one of the idiots, and then it was your playground, assuming of course, you had enough mates with you to get that "warm and fuzzy, we can do anything we want" feeling. Drink and a dozen or so mates are very empowering. *The Jolly Cobblers* and the *Bunch of Grapes*, opposite each other, were both good pubs that served good food during the weekdays and were patronised by office workers during the day, and it must be said, in the evenings, the custom was mostly idiot free, apart of course, at the weekends.

Now, *The Naval Volunteer* and next door, *The Steam Rock* had a totally different clientele. *The Volly* was a rough house all over the weekend. The management allowed in gangs of idiots, their policy being, get the money off them, and the booze down them. Therefore, as most of these people were idiots to begin with, allowing them to pour drinks down their necks indiscriminately only served to magnify the problem. What a surprise, we had mass punch-ups every weekend.

The Steam Rock, however, had good management, certainly for the first few years of its opening. Cathy Dolphin was the first and she was a pleasure to work with. She knew her job inside out and had the personality to carry it, and most importantly, knew what clientele she was looking for and knew how to manage them. If I am right, she was a Sheffield lass from a recently broken marriage with a couple of kids in tow. I put an excellent head doorman in place. Joe was solid, reliable and highly experienced who had worked for me a few years and had proved his worth many times. It's the head doorman at any club or pub that really dictates what the evening is going to be like. If he or now she, gets it wrong, then the night will turn nasty. Of course, Joe would take instructions from our Cathy, but he was the one who stood on the door, sticking his neck out night after night, week after week, having to decide who came in and who did not. If Joe or any other head doorman got it wrong, and nobody gets it right all the time, bearing in mind Joe would be making a thousand decisions a night, it would turn very nasty and be Dodge City inside *The Steam Rock,* as well as outside. Over the decade or so I was associated with *The Steam Rock,* there were two other first-class head doormen after Joe. Wayne, who went on to have his own very successful security company and Kevin. Now Kevin is one of those indestructible people who are never fazed by anything or anyone, and over the years, he had everything thrown at him. He was a fearless head doorman who, no matter whatever happened, would always come up smiling and finding something from a very violent and nasty incident to laugh at. Kevin, it was a pleasure and a privilege to know you.

I cannot move on with my narrative without mentioning one other, who, on looking back these years later, it was a pleasure and privilege to work with. Remember, I have told you that I have rubbed shoulders with the very finest of people. Well, Steve was, and no doubt still is, one of the best. I employed him for a lot of years before he left to start out on his own, and what a success he has made of it. We worked together, Steve was my assistant really and his loyalty and support in so many ways made my life better and safer. I missed Steve when he left; my company missed Steve when he left.

My one enduring memory of our Cathy, as I would call her, was from a time when she was heavily pregnant with her third child, I guessed at the time, she was about eleven months gone! Anyway, there was trouble on the door and fighting had spilled outside. We were all out there trying to control the violence when our Cathy appeared in the middle of this punch up, pushing and shouting at the opposition.

I had kittens!

With other doormen, I surrounded her to protect her overdue lump, when suddenly, the fighting stopped. A well know actor had appeared in the middle of us, the Bristol Theatre Royal is just over the road. Patrick Malahide gave us all a dirty look, then continued on his way, and we continued fighting. Looking back, it is now amusing and brings a smile, but at the time, my heart was in my mouth. Fiercely loyal to her staff and my doormen, she was a good pal. Our Cathy, you were a pleasure to know too.

We cannot leave King Street without revisiting a nasty incident where I ended up being arrested for grievous bodily harm!

Early hours of a Sunday morning, we were sat in the van parked across the street from *The Steam Rock*, when a small confrontation started on the door. The head doorman was not allowing a small group of men in, and the arguing and shouting had started. We decided to attend and give the doormen support and make the opposition realise they were not just confronting a couple of doormen. Usually, this would do the trick and the idiots would wander off issuing the usual threats and abuse.

However, this was one of those times when it all went downhill very, very rapidly. Suddenly, another half dozen or so men appeared and feeling much more confident, these idiots felt they had a better chance to take us on. We were outnumbered, and it was time to close the door! The door was quite a solid affair, no windows for anyone to pull faces at each other through, and briefly, I felt the problem would go away after they had taken a few kicks at the door to show how tough they all were.

The door began to disintegrate before our eyes. First, the bottom half came through, the planking spilling into the reception area, then the top half started receiving their attention. We had little choice but to open the remains of the front door and confront these idiots. If we had delayed, there would have been nothing left of the door.

No door, no choice!

However, I took comfort in the knowledge that there was a camera, one of those new CCTV things, above the door filming the idiots, and on viewing the pictures, the police, if they should become involved, would see that our actions were reasonable.

CCTV, the doorman's friend.

On opening the remains of the door, John was immediately pulled out into the street. To say he was pulled out is not quite accurate, he was literary ripped out and found himself being mauled by a largish group of very nasty men.

We followed, to rescue John. No choice again! We were going to get John back from these men, no matter what.

There was an explosion of violence as we exchanged blows in trying to get to our man. The fighting was brief and over quickly and we led John back into the relative safety of the reception area. It was then, I noticed one of these idiots had somehow landed with his head through the rear window of a car parked nearby, his lower body and legs draping over the boot.

How did that happen?

But you know, with the kinetic forces unleashed during this highly dynamic type of action, it is not surprising that people get injured. And of course, we had no choice. No way were we going to leave John to the mercies of those idiots.

As I have said, we had CCTV, the doorman's friend.

Or had we?

Some moments later, the police arrived after receiving an emergency call from Mike, the manager following our Cathy. Chief Superintendent John Roberts was in attendance. He came over to me saying the ambulance staff could not stop the bleeding from this man's head and that I was under arrest.

I said, "Check the CCTV, it'll support our actions." At that moment, I still felt safe in the knowledge the camera was my get out of jail free card.

As we both viewed the monitor, Mike the manager, another good guy, explained apologetically that the CCTV equipment was the Mark 1 version and would only record a frame of the incident about every six seconds.

My heart began to sink! I knew what was coming, and sure enough, I was right.

The playback showed the initial confrontation on the door. It even showed the door being kicked in. But then, it showed me and the others charging out of the door. Then, just the last couple of frames of the fight, and that was that.

Roberts, who I had known for several years, looked at me, "This doesn't help you, Martyn." He then instructed one of his officers to arrest me.

I spent twelve freezing hours in a police cell at Southmead, thinking to myself, words to the effect "What the frigging hell am I doing here!" and after an interview with a couple highly dubious CID officers, I was bailed. My son-in-law collected me from the station, with me wearing the paper suit I had been issued during the night. The idiots had won this one!

Following what had been a rotten night in the cells with me very cold and feeling sorry for myself, a police sergeant entered my cell. His manner was friendly and asked if I would like some tea. This refreshment was very welcome, and I asked if he had a tissue I could wrap my contact lenses in. He said he was wearing contacts as well and gave me one of his plaster holders to put them in. Thank you, sergeant, your timely visit and friendly manner, and the cup of tea really cheered me up.

Two weeks later, my solicitor received a letter from the CID saying they had received information from two ladies who had witnessed the incident throughout, and I had been exonerated and had no charges to answer. Thank you, ladies, whoever you are.

Well, the kindness of strangers!

This incident though, had left me with a bad taste in my mouth, and really questioning if I had had enough. Already, I had been on the street working the doors and managing night clubs since I was 15 years old. There was so much at risk should I be arrested and convicted of something like this. I had to put my thinking hat on. It is getting close to that time.

Former Sergeant Major Ed, Royal Marines, where are you?

Muscle

I badly needed a change of direction; I could feel myself burning out on the street. I was tired, I was taking knocks and making mistakes, and starting to show my teeth, more than a smile. Not a good place to be in my world. Mind you, I was in my late fifties by then, and the King Street punch-up where I had been arrested had not been the last time that would happen.

Let me explain…….

A notebook and a pencil

It was a Saturday evening late in the last year of the old millennium. Chris, Mike, Ron and I were in the van, dubbed the Battle Bus by the police. We had been back at the office dropping off cash collected from 'door' contracts that still paid in real money. Years before, everyone had paid in cash, but now increasingly, the operators and breweries had wanted just our invoice and we would find ourselves waiting, sometimes weeks, to be paid. There were times when we had paid doormen their monthly salary, VAT and other expenses on the account before we were paid. Many of the smaller firms were effectively put out of business due to this, and I could see a looming cash flow problem if we were not careful.

Mike took a call from the landlady of *The Bunch of Grapes*, the pub in King Street.

King Street again.

Mike sat in the front passenger seat of the van, answering the call. I sat behind him and could hear the agitated and fearful voice of this lady from where I was sitting. She was clearly very disturbed over something.

I listened to Mike's reassuring voice, telling her we were on our way and not to worry.

Mike twisted round in his seat, his face showing concern, "Sounds serious, landlady's very frightened."

Ron replied with a typical Ron leg-pull, "Well let's get there, you knobhead!"

"Mike, tell the landlady to call the police if it's that serious. We'll be there in a few minutes," I said, laughing at Ron. Mike was used to Ron's way.

Anyone who Ron liked would be the constant butt of his jokes and leg-pulls. Never a dull moment with Ron around. It was Ron, my friend of 40 years, that larger than life character, who became the real star of the TV programme *Muscle*.

Keith, our driver, turned the van around and headed for King Street, it was only a few minutes away. We were there in no time and pulled up outside the pub. From the van, I could see through the window into the pub, and what I saw gave me a bad feeling, the sort of feeling you may have experienced before, when suddenly you realise that things were about to go very, very wrong. I slipped off my watch and put it into my trouser pocket, I had lost too many watches in punch-ups to leave this one on my wrist. There was an awful lot of men all bunched up in the bar, and my bad feeling was about to get worse.

The landlady and her husband were standing outside their pub, clearly too frightened to be in their own premises. She looked nervous, and I saw the relief on her face when she saw the van arrive.

The four of us got out of the van, and I asked Keith to drive to the top of King Street and wait there and walked across the pavement to the pub. The landlady took my arm saying "Thank God you're here. They're dreadful people. They have been helping themselves from behind the bar."

Some of you may remember a TV programme at the turn of the millennium titled *Muscle*. Well, two of the main characters in the 6-episode series were Chris and I, with another two characters that had worked for me at the time, Mike and Ron, who were both good friends of mine.

I had known Roy, the producer and director of the programme, over the course of the previous 2 years, and he had been sounding me out about doing a documentary on my security company and how I ran the business.

I finally gave in to his repeated requests, although it must be said, I now regret that decision. But at the time, I was seriously thinking of stepping back from the operational side of the business to pursue other ideas, and I daydreamed that this would be my swansong to the street, never dreaming it would have the impact it had when it was aired in the early months of 2000.

As I stepped into the bar, I saw the barman leaning against the back counter of the bar, a look of fear on his young face. He was stuck to the spot, unable to move, his hands gripping the counter behind him, elbows high almost in line with his shoulders.

I looked across the room, there were probably about twenty men there and it was obvious that they had been making themselves very unpleasant.

Where was the doorman I had there?

It is times such as these when you need to start thinking, if you have time, that is. Think about the options you have and ways to get the problem sorted without getting yourself and those with you in too much peril or trouble, either with the police or the brewery that employs you. The thing about breweries is that they will always blame the door staff or the door company, to get themselves off the hook with the police.

So, here was my choice. Either we could back off and let this mob have their way and wait for the police or go ahead and confront these thugs. The sensible choice should have been to wait for the police. Surely?

I remember looking out of the window wondering where the police were and seeing the licensee and her husband, looking fearfully through the window, then saw Adrian, the doorman, another former police officer who had retired on health grounds. He had asked me for a job to give him some cash flow while he sorted his domestic life out. I gave him *The Bunch of Grapes*, believing it was a soft door and not give him any serious problems.

I got that wrong, as well!

Adrian was standing in the thick of the mob, speaking to three of them. He was a tough one, he was not going anywhere. Adrian was standing his ground in a very frightening situation.

I looked from Adrian to the barman riveted in terror behind his bar and thought of the landlady and her husband outside, too fearful to be in their own pub and said to myself, "FUCK IT!" and stepped into the mob and shouldered my way towards Adrian. Chris, Mike and Ron were at my back, they always were.

"The rest of this mob are manageable, but these three have to go," Adrian said. I looked at him, thinking, I had only put him here because I thought it would be an easy place to work. It was clear that Adrian was up for anything I decided, a look of grim determination on his face.

"Alright Adrian. How you doing?"

"Whatever you say, Mart."

I turned to the three men, who were old enough to know better, not youths, grown men almost certainly with wives and children waiting at home. "Okay, you heard the man, you have to go. Finish your drinks now and leave the premises."

"No, why? We haven't done anything."

How many times had I had to go through this preamble before it got serious? I had had enough of this crap. This idiot was about five ten and stocky with it. The other two idiots were listening with interest.

Umm, they were up for it. Oh dear, here we go again.

"The licensee wants you off the premises," I said, looking into the eyes of the first man. "And you are going to leave one way or the other." I knew if push came to shove, all the others would join in to support their mates.

"No, we're not going anywhere."

"You're now trespassing. Finish your drinks and leave," I repeated.

We had now got the pleasantries out of the way.

I had been in this type of situation a thousand times over the years, and nine times out of ten, idiots will usually take their time finishing their drinks, to show, of course, how tough they are, then leave, uttering threats and the rest of the nonsense.

However, there are times, when despite all your best efforts to facilitate a peaceful outcome, it all blows up in your face.

"You tell me why the licensee wants us out," he said. I saw this idiot had slipped into a pre-dynamic stance, that is a boxer's stance that allows him to launch an attack without further adjustment to the way he is standing.

I knew instinctively an attack was coming.

"I don't know, I don't know. Ask her, she's outside too frightened to come in her own pub," I replied, took his elbow and quickly turned him to the door.

These three idiots erupted into violence.

My problem was I knew that there was a BBC camera crew filming us which was very inhibiting and remember shouting, as much for the camera's sake as anything else, "It doesn't have to happen."

Chris, Mike, Ron, Adrian and I struggled as the others joined in with their thug mates. We grabbed who we could and pushed and pulled them to the pub door.

Going through that door was like a cork being pulled from a bottle, for a moment, I thought the door frame was going to come away as over two dozen were squeezed into an all too small space, then suddenly pop, and we all spilled out into the street.

The five of us become separated, as we were overwhelmed by their superior numbers, and I found myself surrounded by three of them. I backed away, there were a couple of very big men and I wanted more space. They moved with me and closed in. I hit them both hard in their faces and they reeled away, the third backed off. Typical! He didn't like the odds anymore.

I looked across the street and saw running fights between us and these idiots, and then spotted Ron. He was down and encircled by several men. It was only a matter of seconds before he would start to get a kicking, so I ran over to him. I burst through the idiots and pulled Ron to his feet. One of them moved in my direction and I punched him hard in the head and he dropped to the ground. Ron and I backed away as the other idiots gathered themselves and plucked up their courage for another assault on us.

I saw Adrian fighting two men further down the street outside *The Jolly Cobblers* but couldn't reach him at this time, and even more worrying, I didn't know where Chris or Mike were, as there was so much going on.

It was at this time I received a heavy blow to the back of my head. At the time, I thought I had been hit with a piece of wood or a bottle. The blow was not so much painful as it was stunning, and for a few seconds, my senses were thick and confused, but my reactions were still quick as I spun and grabbed the man behind me. Then taking his head, I ran him across the pavement and rammed his head into a waiting wall. The other idiots had followed and attacked. I was knocked to the ground and the kicks started to come in.

Ouch!

My other companions must have seen this as I felt myself being hoisted to my feet and there was the reassuring presence of Chris, Mike, Ron and Adrian. I cannot remember who, but one of them said, "What the fuck was you doing down there?" Excellent! We were still laughing. It's when the laughing stops that it's the time to worry, and we fought these thugs a hard, gritty fight for more than several seconds before they again backed off, and we were able to collect ourselves and get our breath back.

I was later to learn that the BBC film crew had filmed the whole incident and later watched the unedited tape and saw that the blow to my head was in fact a head butt. I hope it hurt that cowardly thug; it certainly gave me a headache.

My memory of the rest of this King Street fight is somewhat sketchy and I have not seen the fight on tape since it was shown on TV in the spring of the new millennium. After writing this account from memory, I think perhaps I had better watch it again, Chris and I often talk about it and compare notes.

Anyway, the police arrived sometime during the final confrontation. I remember seeing the police van arrive and several officers jump out. A police sergeant and a WPC ran over to our position. The WPC had a notebook and pencil in her hand, and both took up position between us and the idiots. It was then the police sergeant arrested me on suspicion of causing grievous body harm.

Here we go again! I thought and shook my aching head in amazement. Across the road, where Ron had been knocked to the ground, lay one of these thugs, presumably the one I had hit. He was surround by police and others, presumably giving him succour and comfort while waiting for an ambulance to arrive.

So, another long cold night in police cells dressed in a paper suit lay ahead. I've had enough of this!

Ed, where are you?

Once again, after the police watched the unedited tape, I was exonerated. A few days later, it was filtered down to us that the police who had watched the tape had shown it to their colleagues and all had thoroughly enjoyed it and started referring to us as the Magnificent Seven. Well, I'm glad they enjoyed the fight, at least.

A couple of years later in Los Angeles, Ed and I were showing the tape of King Street to a bunch of LA County Deputy Sheriffs and they were amazed that I was arrested in the first place and then split their sides laughing on seeing the WPC running over with just a notebook and pencil in her hand.

Chapter 4

Caesar and Cleopatra

I had a phone call from Ed who was working in Haiti, wherever that was. He sounded as though it was urgent.

Hurrah!

"Martyn", his soft Glaswegian tones were music to my ears. "I'm putting together a team for the presidential protection unit here, I want you and Chris here asap. Can you do it at short notice?

My heart sang, and I did not need to think too long. "Yes, and I'm seeing Chris later this morning. I'll email you when I've spoken to him."

"Err, Martyn," there was a moment's hesitation while Ed thought how to put his next few words: "It's dangerous here mate."

It's dangerous here too, Ed,' I thought, smiling to myself. "I need you to know that, we lose our Haitian counterparts for a pastime here. Tell Chris. And put your affairs in order mate."

Ed obviously needed to get that off his chest, and then could always say if I got my arse shot off, "Martyn, I told you so!" We had worked together before in places Ed would describe as shitholes with us as the toilet cleaners, and I was an instructor on Ed's Close Protection courses in Los Angeles.

I always looked forward to a thought provoking, frightening call from Ed.

"Sounds like the money's good, Ed?" And it was.

"Get your arse over here mate, I need you and Chris."

I spent the next few days putting my affairs in order and researching Haiti.

Umm! The Foreign Office website simply said, "Don't go there!"

I flew out a few days later with a night in one of the Miami Airport's hotels, where my room had wallpaper covered with huge bright red, dancing flamingos that kept me awake all night. Every time I opened my eyes, there they were dancing round my room. Then, still tired from the transatlantic flight and hardly any sleep, I caught the early morning ninety-minute flight down to Port au Prince. Chris was due to follow me out, a few days later.

Not really knowing what to expect after reading up on Haiti, and well recalling the bad press Papa Doc Duvalier earned the country during his bloody years as president, I took my seat on the plane with some trepidation. I had learnt over the years to accept my fears and that way, I could begin to manage them. It was a lesson well learnt, for some years later in a very different place, the Taliban were kidnapping everyone they could get their hands on, not only their own countrymen but visiting Europeans working as NGOs, diplomats, engineers and missionaries. There, on local TV stations, a Taliban spectacular would be shown as these poor people had their heads sawn off.

A harrowing sight.

I came to the decision that I would not be taken alive, and so, at night, in my room, I would have a fragmentation grenade in hand's reach, so should all other lethal options fail, we would all go to heaven. Well hopefully, only me, the Taliban could go to hell.

Once I had come to terms with that decision, I was able to function normally.

On landing at Port au Prince, I followed the other passengers across the tarmac to Arrivals and Passport Control, where I stood in line, dutifully and patiently, speculating what the immigration officer would make of me and my British Passport. I wondered if they would had even seen a British passport before. The other passengers seemed to be Haitians returning from the United States; there is a large population of Haitians living there, and white Americans that looked suitably holy, and my suspicion was that they were missionaries, perhaps? I was to learn that an awful lot of young American missionaries worked there, and a regular number would be kidnapped and held for ransom, which their home church in the States would presumably pay.

I was startled by a large smiling Haitian lady who introduced herself as Madame St Pierre, "I am the Diplomatic Director of Port au Prince airport. Please follow me," she said, pirouetting beautifully, stepping off. I followed, intrigued and admiring her light, delicate, finely placed dancer's footwork.

Madame St Pierre waved me through Passport Control without reference to the immigration officer who looked up, saw my escort and looked down again, and continued checking passengers' passports.

Ed's smiling face was waiting for me.

Madame St Pierre instructed me to wait, then said with a lovely smile, "I will arrange for your luggage to be collected. Please give me your luggage ticket." Again, she pirouetted and stepped off like a ballerina.

Ed and I shook hands, pleased to see each other again, it had been some months since Southern California, and then *what the hell,* we embraced like long lost brothers. It was great to see him again.

Ed was 'carrying'. The pistol was holstered in its usual position for Ed, just on the back corner of his right hip, hidden from sight by his Fisherman's Vest.

"This is dodgy here mate." It was good to hear his soft, gentle Glaswegian accent again, "I want you up to speed by the time we reach the door and get to the car." He then went on to brief me on the latest drive-by shootings and various other killings.

Ooh Ahh!

My cases arrived, and Madame St Pierre waived goodbye, flashing me a brilliant, beaming smile. What a lovely lady she was, and I was to interact with her on several occasions during my time in Haiti. One time was when I was collecting President Aristide from a trip he had taken to Cuba. His prime minister, ministers and press were waiting on the tarmac and I needed to get airside, so I'd be waiting by the plane's steps as he exited the aircraft. Being armed was a big no-no, so I contacted this lovely lady and told her my problem. She knew her president's life was constantly in danger, even from some of his closest associates. Madame St Pierre simply said, "Follow me," and she ushered me through the airport officials and members of the government, waving them aside, taking me to the bottom of the steps that President Aristide would shortly being descending. A lovely lady.

I followed Ed through the Diplomatic Lounge and stepped through the entrance where his vehicle was waiting.

Nothing had prepared me for the sensory overload that hit me. It was a bomb blast effect of thousands of people milling about at the airport entrance, and the clamour of sounds this teeming humanity made as it assaulted my ears. Then the smell, as it kicked into my olfactory senses. It was not particularly offensive, but it took some taking in. Overriding all this was the chaos of colour and dirt and rubbish and more rubbish, all mixed brightly together giving anyone not prepared, that overwhelming punch on the nose. It left my eyes watering.

We reached the vehicle by threading our way through this milling mass of folk, rubbish and smells and reached the big old four-wheel drive, a battered land cruiser. I noticed how shabbily dressed the people were: Brightly dressed, but their clothing had seen better days. It was obvious that I was in a very poor country. Ed motioned me into the back, as he climbed into the front next to the driver. He then introduced me to Mark, who nodded, his concentration focused elsewhere and everywhere, and he pulled away without speaking, his hand on the horn aggressively and threateningly making his way through the crowds. It was apparent that this was going to be a very brief introduction as they both obviously did not want to hang around this area making small talk. This was clearly a very dangerous place to be sitting in a car having a chat, and I noticed the two Uzi Sub machine guns in the driver's and front passenger's foot-wells. Ed turned and handed to me a loaded Beretta pistol with a couple of spare magazines. "Arm it and leave it 'hot'." Ed un-holstered his weapon and placed it between his thighs. "Right," I said.

Right! I thought.

The ride from the airport to the Ibo Lele, the hotel some of the team were staying in was eye opening, educational and amazing, and I could not quite take it all in. The sensory assault continued as we turned left and followed the runway for some way then passed the Haitian National Police Tactical Response Unit barracks and on to the former United Nations base and out into the countryside.

"We park the Helos behind there." Ed said.

The UN base had been built some years previously, in fact the last time the US Marines had invaded Haiti and re-instated President Aristide. The base had not been used for years. It was dilapidated, but still clearly showed it had once been a very strong defensive position.

Umm, defending themselves from whom? I wondered. There was a lot to learn about the politics of this country and I had better start learning fast if I was to be of any use, and not get my arse shot off, and I was reminded of the phone conversation Ed and I had had that morning when he made the job offer. Everything had moved so fast since that call and it was increasingly obvious that I needed to get up to speed very, very quickly.

As we left the airport and the urban areas behind, I could sense both my companions start to relax.

"Pleased to have you on board Martyn, Ed's told me all about you, Mark commented. This is the roundabout way to the Ibo Lele, safer than driving through Port au Prince."

I guessed Mark had been sent by their boss Derek to give me the once over and make sure I looked the part. Americans I was to learn put a lot in store by people 'looking the part.' That is their euphemism for looking tough, being armed to the teeth and very quickly in any likely confrontation or threat going to guns immediately.

"Helos, Ed?" I asked frowning.

Yeah, when we move the president from the National Palace to his residence. Or anywhere else for that matter. We'll pass Cactus shortly."

"Cactus?

Mark laughed, "You'll have nothing but questions for the first few weeks. I know I did."

"White House and Cactus are the code names for the National Palace and his private residence. He stays at the White House during the week, then we move him and the family on Friday evenings to Cactus. His code name is Caesar, the first lady is Cleopatra and the two kids are Dancer and Prancer. We have 'top cover' when we move them. One of us giving advance intel, and one of our snipers.

"Right". I replied. Right! I thought.

Chapter 5

Flag Day

The tip of my tie was dripping wet. It had taken some time for me to realise where the drips that were leaving dark patches on my trousers were coming from. I felt the rest of the tie, it was sopping wet, leaving a small liquid pool in my sweating palm. My shirt collar was soaking, and the rest of the shirt was stuck to my body under the jacket.

The belt holding up my trousers was uncomfortably tight and causing the inner waistband to stick to my itching waist. It had to be tight, as it was carrying my pistol, fully loaded and 'hot' with sixteen rounds and waiting in its holster, four spare fifteen round magazines in their holsters, an Asp in its case, a Seal Pup knife in its sheaf, attached to my belt laying horizontal in the small of my back, its handle just behind my left hip in easy reach, and finally, my personal radio.

Usually I would wear a duty belt when not formally dressed, that would comfortably carry all that stuff, but even then, after wearing it for twelve hours, it would start to suck. Later, I bought a shoulder holster for when we had to be suited and booted like today, and the relief was exquisite. A fully loaded pistol and spare mags is heavy, and the longer you carry all that stuff, the heavier it gets.

Using the loo with all that iron around your waist is a laugh if you are not too desperate, as your sweat soaked trousers will drop like a stone from your waist as soon as you unbuckle the belt. Trying to pull them up again is pretty well impossible; you must unload all the iron first, otherwise, as soon as you take your hands off the trousers' waistband to re-buckle the belt, everything plummets back to earth again. You could spend hours in the loo just trying to pull your trousers up! And what is more, do not think that if you were to slightly bend your knees, gentlemen, it would give you time to make a grab for the belt buckle. Oh no, that will not do, your trousers will still plunge back to earth, only this time, they will have turned inside out! Keep laughing!

Too much bloody stuff.

As usual, I found myself carrying too much equipment, but then again, I would argue with myself, what was the point of having a choice of weapons and then leaving some of that choice behind? The logic was that it's better looking at them, or in my case, carrying them, than looking for them. Anyway, there was an awful lot of iron hanging from my waist, and it was dragging my trousers slowly but surely down. All in all, I was very uncomfortable.

At the time, I was standing on a large podium behind two huge high-backed regal, no, throne-like chairs, where President Aristide and the First Lady Madame Aristide were seated. However, I was not looking out from the podium at the thousands of Haitians facing the stage, all clamouring to get close enough to pass messages to their president. On walkabouts, he would collect hundreds of small pieces of paper with pleas for help and mobile phone numbers for him to call. I never did find out what happened to these pieces of paper, there must have been sack loads somewhere in his office suite. My attention on that podium was focused on the hundred or so members of his government, Police chiefs and other dignities seated behind their president. Even the police, we disarmed when entering the presence of the president. He had deadly enemies in all strata of Haitian society.

Ed and Chris were standing at the front of the stage with others facing out. At least they were standing in the open air, as this podium had a coloured plastic roof designed to protect from the tropical sun. But for those seated or stood like me well back from the edge of the podium and fresh air, this roof had created a microclimate of stifling heat and humidity. I was sweating buckets. It was pouring out of me. I was seriously leaking.

There were four of us on the security advance party. It was Flag Day in Haiti, their national day, celebrating the 1802 revolution when Haitians threw off the heavy yoke of French colonialism. Our job was to enter and secure the town of Archiai, making sure there was nothing nasty waiting for President Aristide on his arrival. The town is on Haiti's northern claw about a two hour drive from Port au Prince on Haitian roads, and where, during the 1802 uprising, one of the town's women pulled down the French flag, the Tricolour and ripped out the white part from between the blue and the red and sewed it together again forming the beginnings of the very attractive Haitian national flag it is today. Every year on Flag Day the Haitian President and his government visit this lady's grave and celebrate when Haiti, which is roughly half of the fabled island of Hispaniola became the world's first Slave Nation.

My most vivid memory of that day was when the four of us arrived early morning, a couple of hours before the presidential motorcade was due to arrive. Ed, Chris, Mark and I were dressed in suits, shirt, collar and ties, showing dutiful respect to this day and the Haitian people. It was still reasonably cool when Mark parked our vehicle just outside the town's main square and gave a smiling young boy a five-dollar bill and told him to watch the vehicle saying in Haitian patois, there would be another on our return. This lad had never seen so much money, his wide-eyed smile grew wider, and the four of us walked into the square.

Archiai has a large square for what is a relatively small provincial town some fifty miles west from the capitol. To our left at the top of the square is the town's cathedral that overshadows and dominates the other buildings in the square, its Bell Tower over the main entrance is where Ed would shortly site our counter snipers. It would be comforting to know they would be covering us if it all went south in the square. Opposite, at the other side of the square is the town hall, and down both sides a range of single, and one-story buildings, good cover for any attackers, which reminds me of an amusing story I must tell.

Although us Brits and Americans sort of speak the same language it does not always translate correctly. Let me explain. One day we had an exercise on clearing buildings, that's running into a building or house and neutralising any armed bad guys. Gale, who was running the exercise, shouted "First Floor!"

And so, all us Brits ran upstairs. Gale shouted, "I said First Floor!" Us Brits shouted back "This is the fucking first floor!" Of course, for Americans the first floor is the ground floor, and the first floor is the second floor to them.

Confused? We worked it out. Something else to laugh at when having a beer at the end of the working day.

Although it was early in the day there was at least a couple of thousand people gathered waiting for their president to arrive as us four Blancs made our appearance.

We walked into the square line abreast, and there came an audible hush as the sound of two thousand chattering voices suddenly stopped as they became aware of our presence, the hum and buzz of voices and movement quickly fading away into a heavy silence. People stood and stared at the four of us, who were to them, creatures from a different world, another planet even. Most of these folks probably had rarely seen a white person before.

The atmosphere became very tense, not so much intimidating, but as if aliens had just landed in the town, and all the curiosity, phobia and natural discrimination that event would bring. After all, it was their National Day celebrating the overthrow of a European Superpower as Napoleon's France had been, and to be frank it was obvious that we Blancs were not welcome.

The walk into the town square brings the image of Wyatt Earp, his brothers with Doc Holliday on their legendry walk to the OK Corral to mind. I of course, stuck out my chest and began quietly chanting to my companions, "Chin up, chest out, plenty of swagger."

It was a might unsettling though.

To be honest, we were very exposed, and each of us knew that if these folk decided they did not want "White Devils" coming to their town on Flag Day there was not a lot we could have done about it, and following a very brief but bloody melee there would be nothing much left to bury as these country folk's weapon of choice is the machete! After all, white is the Voodoo colour of death.

The thought of that gruesome execution still gives me the shudders. It would have been an awful death. I would much prefer to die of old age! But as usual, Chris and I were to find as we grew to understand these wonderful people, that after the surprise of seeing us they continued about their business with their natural dignity and reserve, and I had the comfort in knowing that I was with a couple of the finest people one could hope for in a "tight spot".

Ed with his former life in the Royal Marines, ending his career as a senior NCO, his combat experience and as a former police officer, and not least, he is Glaswegian. Ed and I would find us working closely together again sometime later in another place, the other side of the world. Nothing more needs to be said about Ed, except for an incident a couple of years after Haiti, that really sums up my friend's character and demonstrates what a pleasure it was to work with him.

We were in Kurdistan where there are parts of this disputed region, that really are the end of the world, and to understand something of the atmosphere hanging over this town, you must know that not only were all Kurds in dispute with the Iraqi national government wanting their country back after it had been wiped off the maps when the British back in the early thirties redrew the map dividing up the nation of Kurdistan between Iraq, Turkey, Syria and Iran. Plus, this region, now known as Northern Iraq Kurdistan, has two powerful and warring tribes, the Talabani, (Nothing to do with the Islamic terror group, the Taliban) and the Barzani. Each had been slaughtering each other for centuries. Our drivers were Barzani, and we were in the tribal lands of the Talabani.

We were body guarding a senior European consultant engineer whose company was overseeing the replacement and refurbishment of all the power lines and towers throughout Northern Iraq. We had taken him to a mountain town that again was really at the end of nowhere. Sulimaniyah did not welcome Europeans, although there was no open hostility shown to us, but we sensed a very real threat. Apart from the locals who did not want us there as regular attacks by Al-Qaeda and another terror group who called themselves the Army of God, would target the Hotels, especially the ones any Europeans stayed in, especially the Americans who had a heavy CIA presence in the town, and an airfield a short distance away.

Enter Ed and I with our client Rudolph Fitchner, who had travelled from Stuttgart for an arranged meeting with the local Talabani government minister.

On entering the hotel, we were faced with dozens of hostile looks from the men there. These locals were clearly demonstrating that they were not happy with our presence. The atmosphere became very tense, smelt of damp clothing, and was thick with tobacco smoke from their cheap Turkish cigarettes. No women, just men drinking chia, a sweet tea, and frowning at us with their thick bushy eyebrows that for most men there met in the middle of their foreheads reflecting in size and colour of their thick moustaches.

We were both carrying our usual armoury, but because of the threat level in the town we were both carrying our AK Assault Rifles.

Ed showed Heir Fitchner to the waiting minister and stood guard over our charge, he was eyes on our principle, the local minister and those seated nearby. I stood a short distance away with the entrance and exits in my eye line but facing the frowning, chain smoking, chia drinkers who continued their staring, and I asked myself if they had ever heard of or knew anything of etiquette! Did they not know it was rude to stare? I looked back at them, an expressionless, casual look on my face, the Bodyguard's thousand-yard stare, belying what was going on in my head.

A while later, Ed wandered over to me and said in his usual quiet Glaswegian tones, "Do you know what would clear this place quicker than a Frag' Grenade?" I shook my head, gripping my AK tighter taking comfort in the feel of cold gunmetal and happy at this distraction. Ed smiled and answered his own question, "A bar of soap!"

The tension in our bodies was released by this urgently need humour and we both stood there laughing at each other much to the bemusement of the locals.

Then there is Chris, he and I had been in, and would in the future find us standing back to back and being very glad of each other's company. Indeed, not a couple of hours later after mass in the cathedral, we were back to back "on the door" again controlling entry to the president's reception in the grounds of the cathedral. There was a lot of people who thought they could browbeat and shoulder their way in. We would turn to Orial the president's Chief of Intelligence and raise our eyebrows and he would either nod or shake his head. A shake of the head would result in a bit of pushing and shoving.

The four of us Blancs began our walk round the square, firstly to shown ourselves to the waiting crowds, that told these folks that President Aristide was on his way, secondly to see if we were going to be shot at. That would have given us a clue and confirmed we were not welcome, and for us to warn our other team escorting the president and the first lady to stay out of town. I checked under the podium looking for any packages labelled BOMB! It was a big area and it was dark under there, but I took my time and checked it thoroughly, after all I knew I was later to stand on it for some hours. Then we four, still under the gaze of thousands made our way to the cathedral steps where with the bishop, his priests, and other town officials stood waiting for their president's arrival.

The motorcade escorting President Aristide and the first lady swept into the square. Immediately, the natural buzz of sound from thousands of people was turned up to full volume, and they surged towards the cathedral steps with local police trying to hold them back. His big black land cruiser stopping at the bottom of the cathedral steps. Three Blancs and three Haitians scrambled out the two chase vehicles and surrounded His vehicle, the team leader looking at Ed waiting to be given the signal that it was safe for the president and the first lady to alight from their vehicle.

Safe is a relative term used in these situations, and certainly as far as this head of state was concerned. Moving a principle from a vehicle and into a building especially as your principle passes through a doorway is a very risky manoeuvre. Jean Bertram Aristide, a former parish priest had come to power some years previously and had been ousted in a brief and bloody revolution, and then reinstated following a presidential order issued by Bill Clinton to the Caribbean Division of the US Marine Corps to invade. The US, finds itself invading Haiti at least once a decade to stop the bloodshed, restore order and feed the population while it recovers from chaos.

The old Haitian mulatto establishment had lost all their power and influence when Aristide had been elected to the presidency, and following His disbanding of the army, the source of the establishment's power they had plotted his death and the overthrow of his government ever since. There was a constant and very real threat to his life, and the life of the first lady, and the lives of their children.

The whole Aristide family was under a death sentence by the former Duvalists and disaffected members of the establishment and former army officers. We were a very thin line that stood between them and their killers and the chaos that would bring. He could not completely trust his own Secret Service, too many of his enemies with too much money that would quickly turn the heads of his Haitian bodyguards. At that time there was only eleven of us Blancs guarding him twenty-four seven against these dark forces.

We had satisfied ourselves that there was no obvious or immediate threat waiting for him at this location at this time. That of course could and would change in a blink of an eye, and Ed had placed our counter snipers in the bell tower overlooking the cathedral steps and the square. But as ever, there is really no answer to the lone-wolf gunman, waiting in the crowd for their opportunity to spray the whole area the president is in with a Machine Pistol such as the old Ingrams that were carried by security guards on the entrance doors of the few supermarkets, night clubs and restaurants in Port au Prince. The Ingram is an ideal weapon for an assassin hiding in a crowd. The weapon is easily hidden under clothing and more than capable of hosing down targets and everyone else in range with its hundred round magazines in a few seconds. With the chaos an attack like that would cause it would be relatively easy for them to make their escape. On walkabouts with Caesar that thought was always on my mind.

Ed nodded "Clear" and the president's close in bodyguard opened the rear door of his vehicle and he stepped out. Another of our men had covered the other rear door, now opened it and Madame Aristide stepped out and walked round the back of the vehicle and joined her husband. Together, they greeted the waiting luminaries as they climbed the steps up to the doors of the cathedral, turned and waved at the surging, excited mass of people now totally filling the square. There must have been by then ten thousand people in the square.

Jean-Bertram Aristide, President of the Republic of Haiti is a slight man, probably in his late forties or maybe early fifties some five foot four inches tall. A naturally smart dapper man with a slight turn in one eye. His movements are quick, bird-like, and when he decides to go in another direction, he would turn quickly catching you unawares. You had to keep him constantly in your peripheral vision otherwise you would lose him from your sight. Not a good place to be having to ask, "Where did he go?". "You lost the president!" There was one time when He was visiting a patient in Port au Prince Hospital, one of his Haitian security team had been shot in the head during an incident. I was then his close-in bodyguard and suddenly, he darted from one room to another. I had eyes on an uncovered zone and had not seen this and turned back to find him gone. Oh shit! I really have lost the president!

But it was alright, Chris again was covering my back and had followed him. Caesar needed to be constantly somewhere in your vision while covering all the other stuff. It was fine when he felt threatened or we had a contact, he would stick to me like glue, on one occasion looking up at me with the beginnings of fear in his eyes saying and understating the immediate danger we were both in "I would like to go now".

"Yes," I thought, "So would I mate!"

Now Mildred Aristide, the first lady and a former New York lawyer would be very nervous at times and would look at me with timorous eyes telling me she did not want to be wherever we were at the time. Either taking her with Dancer and Prancer to ballet or piano class, visiting schools, the hospital, but mostly Saturday mornings, I would find myself as her personal bodyguard to take her to funerals and on occasions to a supermarket in Port au Prince to buy shopping to cook the president a wifely dinner. Open topped coffins as the first thing on Saturday mornings is not recommended, not in the tropics. On an occasion at the supermarket, she was recognised by two downtown gang members and they started demanding money from her. She had the children with her and went to her purse to give them money. I had other ideas and pulled my Asp and rapidly delivered to them the good news. I could see the relief in her eyes as I got her and the kids safely to the waiting vehicle. She and the children had been very frightened by these two idiots. She profusely thanked me, and I like to think she would have invited me to dinner that evening if protocol had allowed it.

I've digressed again. I apologise.

So, apart from the loss of most of my body fluid on the podium there is another enduring memory of that day in Archiai. Voodoo dancers!

I think they were men and women there, although it was hard to be certain as they were all dressed in white from top to toe. White tops with long white sleeves, and white skirts down to and almost covering their bare feet. On their heads, were tall white conical hats. There must have been a dozen or so of them. They danced to the beat of drums played by others again all dressed in white. Remember, this is a Voodoo nation, yes Haiti is Roman Catholic and the people are very religious, but the influence of Voodoo is stronger. Haitians were taken as slaves from West Africa, mostly Sierra Leon and Guinea where still, they will tell you is their spiritual home and were Voodoo is feared and followed.

The dancers were perfectly synchronised as if they were somehow under the control of a master puppeteer. The dancing was elemental, ancient body gyrations straight out of Africa, something quite primeval. I can still see the dust swirling about them as they danced and stamped their feet on the square's hard ground. The image has never left me.

Following the podium and a brief walk to the grave of the flag lady, the president and the bishop and priests walked through the crowds towards the bishop's house, I cannot describe the bishop's residence as a palace, it was a house, the type Americans call a gingerbread house. Walking through those people, thousands of them, everyone felt very exposed and not helped by "Intel" from our Haitian counterparts, "They are here." "Who the hell are They"? we would ask, and with a shrug of their shoulders they would reply "Them." There was always something about Haiti you could not quite put your finger on. All smoke and mirrors! And as the saying goes, "Believe nothing you hear, and only half of what you see."

I was close-in to the president and first lady on this walk, with the others of our detail making an amorphous circle round us. But it did not feel right, and I was tense waiting for an attack. It is amazing how alive you feel when waiting for and expecting deadly force to be used against you. Your built-in radar not missing a sparrow's blink. Your instinct, that primal survival mechanism constantly feeding you information and insights of your surroundings.
I feathered my fingers over the pistol at my left hip, seeking its reassurance. It was fully loaded and 'hot', that means there was a bullet already in the breach, all I needed to do was squeeze the trigger and the weapon would go bang. But you know, despite knowing that there was a round in the breach, there was a little ritual I would have go through every time I was on mission. I would rack back the slide to exactually see the round in the breach. I was not satisfied until I saw it.

"Sparrow?" the voice was coming from my earpiece, it was Jimmy Ryefinger, one of our snipers, a former US Marine Corp gunnery sergeant, from his position in the church bell tower. I clicked my earpiece speak button twice to tell him I was listening. He continued "Sparrow, what do you feel when through your 'scope you see your target's head turn into pink mist?" I had to answer this, I was intrigued, and pressed the speak switch and said, "No Finger, what the fuck do you feel?" Jimmy replied in his beautiful southern Kentucky drawl, "Just the recoil son, just the recoil." I waved a hand above my head, giving him the thumbs up and feeling the tension flowing from my body. Others in the detail heard the exchange and gave a loud whoop! Ooh Ahh!

That was pretty well the conclusion of a long day and following his meeting with the bishop we escorted him and the first lady back to their vehicle and watched the motorcade sweep out of the square on its way back to Port au Prince. The square was almost empty now, the crowds having left, and that emptying showing up the tons of rubbish, black plastic bags and empty plastic bottles. In the overcrowded shanties in and around Port au Prince the poor Haitian folk would defecate in the black plastic bags and throw the bags onto their roofs, there was nowhere else to put them. The four of us walked back to our vehicle and the smiling young boy still guarding it. There was an expectant look of his cherub like face and his smile did get wider when Mark handed him another five-dollar bill.

In our vehicle, waiting for us in a cold box were a pile of tightly packed plastic bottles of drinking water. Mercy!

Chapter 6

The White House

The National Palace, code name 'The White House', at night, could be spooky, once the dozens of palace staff had left for the day and a silence settled over the stairs and walkways, corridors, the empty rooms and the two large reception salons. The salon rouge, was where late one evening, the murderous Papa Doc Duvalier dressed in the robes of an Oughan, a Voodoo priest, had summoned his government, the police and army chiefs and staring at them menacingly, surrounded by members of the Tonton Macoute, told his audience that he was the Chief Oughan, while they sat and listened in terror.

And so, as the evenings turned dark, I always had the uncanny feeling that the silence was not just a quietness that happens when buildings empty, but something else I could never quite put my finger on. The Haitian Secret Service, our counterparts, stayed in their quarters on the ground floor, never to be seen patrolling any part of the palace or the grounds and the palace guard force were either nervously staring into the darkness or fitfully dozing in their sangers. No one in Haiti welcomed the night, so at least when patrolling the palace, I would not have to worry about bumping into one of our counterparts in the dark who would fire first and ask questions later, if there was a later.

Me, Ed and Chris would arrive at 1900 and relieve the day team usually numbering six and they would return to the Ebo Lele in the vehicles we had arrived in. Then, should one or both of the president's young children have piano lessons, I would wait downstairs by the lift doors leading to his apartments and usually it would be Madame Aristide who would step from the lift with her girls, code named Dancer and Prancer.

The first lady would smile her recognition of me and ask, "Are they here?" Considering our counterparts were almost always late, I would still, hopefully, be able to answer, "Yes Ma'am," and turn my head to the vehicle behind ours.

It was a short distance to the piano teacher's house which I cannot much describe because as I recall, I only ever visited it in the dark and there is no street lighting in Port au Prince. It was a pleasant terraced house in a street of pleasant terraced houses. We drove in silence, no sirens or red lights, our drivers doing their best to stay under the radar unnoticed while the children in the back sat quiet and watchful sensing their mother's unease. There was always someone watching, someone waiting.

On arrival, the piano teacher would be waiting at her door, a pleasant elderly lady who would speak French, not Haitian creole when greeting the children, then speak to Madame Aristide in the familiar using her Christian name that left me wondering if she had been the first lady's piano teacher when she was a child.

I would wait quietly and impatiently while these pleasantries were over, then ushering them all into the house, ordering one of my counterparts to remain by the front door. I'd then swiftly move through the house and into the back garden satisfying myself our piano teacher had no nasty visitors hidden, then post my counterpart from the front door to the garden door, look him in the eyes telling him or her to remain and I would return to the entrance door leaving it ajar, and stand post in the small front garden.

It was normally about an hour before the family would begin to gather themselves and prepare to leave and as I now recall those evenings, I cannot remember ever listening to Dancer or Prancer playing the piano, for my thoughts and concentration was elsewhere and thinking through the 'what ifs'. For me, it was an anxious hour knowing that several times a week, this visit to the piano teacher would be repeated giving their enemies opportunity to plan and scheme this young family's assassination.

Not on my watch!

The need was to be seen to be proactive. Always being watched, I would pull out from the counterpart's vehicle the remaining men and post them at both ends of the street. They were mostly unhappy and some resentful at having to leave their warm vehicle and enter the darkness and so, on occasions, I would growl my encouragement and visit them often to keep their courage up.

On movement from inside the house, I would enter, nod to the counterpart at the garden door who would return to his vehicle and I would escort the first lady and the children to their vehicle, whose driver had remained behind the wheel. He was a trusted retainer of the Aristide family who had stayed with them when they had fled Haiti some years earlier during the last revolution. I would see the family safely into the vehicle then call softly to the counterpart at the end of the street to get quickly back to his vehicle then get in the family's vehicle, signal the driver to proceed hoping our counterparts in the vehicle behind did not forget to pick up the other counterpart waiting at the top of the street.

After seeing the family met by their butler and safely into the lift, I would radio Ed in our CP (meaning command post) and report my return, then visit Chris, who would be posted up on the second-floor walkway (to our American cousins it was the third floor) at the back of the president's apartments for a chat and to kill some time.

Chris had found himself a not uncomfortable chair to sit on from the salon rouge. This vantage point gave excellent coverage all the way to the rear gate of the palace. He would sit in shadow but still have a couple of dark green camouflage stripes diagonally across his face. White faces can stand out like dim headlights in the gloom and darkness. White, sweaty faces glisten in bright moonlight and so something as simple as a couple of dark stripes over your face can break up the headlamp effect.

A sturdy, if unspectacular FN automatic rifle lay was across his knees, never propped up against the wall lest it slid and clattered down onto the tiled walkway giving his position away to any watcher. On the front line, a long range weapon was just the thing for covering the parade ground, rear gate and that most isolated sanger of all, the palace sangers next to the former and haunted ruins of Duvalier's prison and where I was to spend some hours dodging bullets during an attack on the palace.

There we would sit and chat for a couple of hours, talking of home and our future, sometimes I would call my wife if the timing was right and I would catch up on the family and especially my growing grandsons. But always, I needed to remind myself to be in the zone and not allow my mind to wander. Lack of concentration and complacency is the silent killer in these situations. I would always be conscious of that heightened awareness that excites all one's senses, not forgetting the most primal defence mechanism we all have, our sixth sense or instinct. I have ever been aware that this sense, one which I am pleased to say, is very well developed in me had, on several occasions, alerted me to imminent danger and repeatedly saved me from injury or worse.

Chris and I would share a chocolate bar and from my day sack, pore out a small mug of coffee each from the flask I would fill when on night duty, every few minutes moving slightly, to stay out of the bright moonlight before it was time for me to commence my patrol through the palace corridors and down the rear stairs and into the palace grounds.

It was patrolling alone at night, whether at the palace or his private residence, that I really enjoyed. It was when I could call on all my sixth sense to keep me safe. Of course I would be armed to the teeth with my M16 assault rifle 'hot', locked and loaded with thirty rounds of 5.56mm with six spare magazines in the pockets of my tac vest, plus all my other weaponry and radio that would be constantly speaking softly in my ear as Ed, clucking and worrying about me like an old mother hen would be asking for a sit-rep.

I would move slowly from shadow to shadow lightly stepping in my new boots from the US. The Danners were and still are, the most comfortable boots I have ever worn. The original soles were of soft rippled rubber, allowing me to move in almost silence. I called them my creeping boots and I still have and use them today when at work, although I have had them re-soled some three times up to now.

It was never quite comfortable patrolling the building itself as I found the gloom and deep, dark shadows too still and that stillness and deep silence unsettling, so I would find myself reciting the rhyme, "Sticks and stones can break my bones, but ghosts will never hurt me," and take comfort in the sensuous feel of my rifle and complete my patrol of the building and return to the CP and Ed for another cup of coffee and chocolate before leaving for a walk round the palace grounds.

The CP was a large room on the first floor with two large tables and easy chairs and the radio equipment. It had recently been repaired and redecorated following an earlier attack where the walls and ceiling had taken several hundred rounds of gunfire stripping off areas of plaster work and of course taking out several windows. I would constantly remind myself to stay away from the windows even though at night, in the dark, the ceiling lights would be turned off, leaving only the warm glow of computer screens.

Ed was sat at the CP desk, his face eerily illuminated by the laptop screen in front of him, "Chris okay?" and I would nod my confirmation and ask, "You want coffee, Ed?" and move over to the fridge for the milk and ground coffee. I could never eat on nights, sandwiches and other snacks just did not go down late at night, so I would have coffee and a couple of bars of chocolate to keep my sugar levels up and stop me from falling asleep, hopefully. Surprisingly, Cadbury's milk chocolate could be found in one of the two or three supermarkets in our area of Port au Prince.

As I again struggled into my tac vest and prepared myself mentally to patrol the palace grounds, Ed stood, closed his laptop and began to put on his tac vest and picked up his Uzi. Ed would invariably join Chris on the walkway while I was out patrolling. It gave me, not for the first time, that warm and fuzzy feeling knowing that should things go wrong for me in the grounds, I would have covering fire as I scarpered back inside the palace.

Ed held out his tin of camouflage cream and I dipped two fingers into the cream, spread my fingers and smeared them across my face from my right temple, over my eyes and nose down to my left jaw, "How do I look, dear?"

Ed smiled, "You'll do. Let's do it," and I followed him to the door.

"I'll do the front gates first," I said and stepped down the flight of stairs as Ed climbed up to the second-floor landing and stepping out onto the balcony overlooking the front lawn and both gates, his parting advice coming to my ears, "Watch yourself, mate."

I entered the short tunnel and out to the front of the palace and stopped to say hello to the two palace guards to my left manning the 50-cal machine gun and not for the first time, wondered how many rounds it would fire before jamming. It had been placed there following an attack where a lorry had rammed through one of the two main gates to my left and entered the palace grounds, the gunmen firing off hundreds of rounds with the presidential protection units and palace guard force only able to return fire with rifles and pistols. I was not sure this 50-cal was going to be the answer to that form of dynamic attack with a heavy vehicle and two palace guards that were probably untrained and the gun itself hardly ever cleaned. Should this have happened at night again, the three of us would have closed on the presidential apartments, screamed over our radios for help from the rest of our unit back at the Obu Lele and fought the attack from there.

Probably not the best of outcomes as our re-enforcements would take time organising themselves and get going and probably come under attack themselves getting to the palace. Our counterparts, if they had any sense, would have vanished into the night.

Lovely!

However, these thoughts did help to keep one awake on night duty.

I moved to the left towards the iron railings keeping in the shadow of bushes and trees until I reached the railings, then turned to my right following the fence line down to the sanger. This was probably the most dangerous part of the patrol, as it took me to the furthest point of the grounds in an exposed location and should anyone be lying in wait for a target, they only had to stick their weapon through the railings and pull the trigger.

The other very real problem was when approaching these sangers particularly in the dark was somehow alerting the fearful guards in the sanger and not to shock them into opening fire when you appeared.

I would crouch down a few yards away and whistle softly alerting the guard then whisper enough for him to hear, "Packy problem."

The guard would answer, "Packy problem." and I would hear the relief in his voice and then enter the sanger and spend a few minutes chatting to and reassuring the guard with my presence.

The mobile in my tac vest pocket would then hum softly and tremble as Ed would confirm he had had me covered. It was usually well after midnight by now, so we obeyed radio silence and used our mobiles.

"Okay, Ed, I'm about to return to the palace by the same way, back through the tunnel and out of the far tunnel." That would avoid me having to pass in front of the palace and be silhouetted against its white facade.

The whole business of checking the guards in these two front of palace sangers would easily take well over an hour but having Ed overviewing me was very comforting and would always think to myself with a wry smile, "Now for the easy part," knowing for most of the time, I would be out of sight from Chris and Ed on the second-floor walkway.

Another call from Ed would tell me he was on the high walkway with Chris waiting for me to appear after I had walked down the side of the palace. This walk from the front to the back was in particularly dark shadow and in heavy vegetation, so as I entered the shadow, I would stop for a few minutes to let my pupils adjust to the heavy darkness before moving on.

Then past the carp ponds to my left and garages to the right where still housed, there was the big American saloon gas guzzler that had belonged to Papa Doc. Probably everyone was still too terrified of the long dead monster to touch it.

Walking slowly through the formal gardens where the president would hold garden parties for visiting dignitaries and where his private helicopter would land, I would smell the stench of rotting food outside the kitchens from some distance but would have to pass by to reach the sanger at the back. At night, the guards reply to my greeting would be muted so not to excite the spirits lurking in the shadows. Normally, there were two guards here and only one in the sanger by the prison. Perhaps that posting at night was a punishment.

The main rear gate, always full of street children at night, all sleeping on the ground inside and outside, always left me with a sense of impotence, unable to do anything to help these lost children, there was just too many of them. So dear reader, to be painfully honest, I would close my eyes and try to cleanse the images and thoughts from my mind.

Looking back now, I have been left with a sense of guilt and try to console myself and find solace in the belief there was nothing I could have done.

The sense of guilt never fades though.

And so, leaving the prison sanger until at last, I would turn left when coming out of the rear gate and with some trepidation, walk past the entrance of the prison and stop at the corner where the building ended and again, whistle softly alerting the guard to my presence and calling, "Packy problem."

The guard would step to the sanger's entrance and answer, "Packy problem." Not for the first time I would think, *Sooner or later, the bad guys would cotton on to this recognition signal and I would walk into a world of pain.*

The low wall running away to the right of this sanger was the most exposed and soft underbelly of the palace grounds. Nevertheless, this position still had only one guard who would spend his shift in fear of the prison next door with its dreadful atmosphere, all alone, waiting for an attack at the weakest point of the palace's defences. Maybe it was a manning problem, but someone in the chain of command had not thought through this location? One man, in fear of the dark and all the terrors the dark holds for these very spiritual people and he's going to take to his heels at the first imagined visit from the Voodoo spirits. The only NCO's I ever saw day and night were in the rear gate office.

My empathy was with the guard force whose ageing rifles looking like relics from before World War Two, had probably not be fired, cleaned or serviced for years, and the very limited amount of ammunition issued was almost certainly useless. So I would spend a few minutes with this guard, offering him some chocolate and refusing his offer of a cigarette before walking back across the empty parade ground, which during the day, would be full of parked cars and wandering chickens, through the inner gate next to the garages and into the inner grounds of the palace and look up to see Chris and Ed on the walkway above me.

Now, well into the small hours, the three of us would rotate the rest of our shift with standing post on the walkway for an hour at a time. I would use my next two hours down time by laying stretched out on one of the tables, my day sack for a pillow, a beach towel for a blanket and would doze.

At dawn, the three of us would stand to for a few minutes, two on the walkway and the other on the balcony at the front of the palace watching the gardeners, cleaners and kitchen staff arrive for their day's early start, then retire back to the CP, drink more coffee and wait for the day team to arrive. At the palace, I always found that if I could keep myself busy for the first half of the shift, the rest would slip by quickly enough.

On the drive back to the Ebo Lele, Ed would insist on driving, probably in the knowledge that

Chris or I would nod off behind the wheel. Although not far, there were places, especially on Canopy Verde, passing between shanties either side of the road, where it was prudent to have 'guns up!'

Finally, arriving back at our hotel sometime round 0800, grabbing our kit and weapons and walking straight down a flight of stairs and out into the open air again and the restaurant, I was hungry having not eaten since the early evening before and unable to sleep with nothing left in my stomach.

The problem here was if there should be any young travellers or missionaries having breakfast. Young travellers did not call themselves tourists anymore, they were now travellers, most I thought, kids just finished high school or college from the USA and Canada looking for adventure before starting jobs. The missionaries were easy to spot, fresh, serious faces, smart suits and white shirts, mostly young and innocent with gullible expressions and bibles on the table beside them.

Then we would arrive, looking as if we had just stepped in from a battle zone, dripping with weapons and this look could cause alarm. The three of us would put our rifles on the floor and greet them all, going from table to table, shaking their hands and reassuring everyone. The young travellers greeted us with questions and wonder, the missionaries I felt looked at us as if we were demons from hell.

Finally, sitting at our favourite table close to the tall palm trees, Camey, our waiter, would be bringing us over a large jug of coffee and typically French breakfast coffee cups and saucers, pour each of us a cup and stand ready to take our orders.

Heaven.

We would spend an hour or so over breakfast then say in schoolboy humour, 'Goodnight' to each other, often repeating this old worn out joke before retiring to our rooms.

Once alone in my room, there was a fastidious ritual I would just have to go through before finally getting into bed.

Let me explain chronologically.

First, I would lay my rifle on the table, take the pistol from its holster on my tac vest and put it in the holster on my duty belt, it would now remain in hand's reach whenever I was in the bedroom, dressing room or bathroom.

I'd listen at the connecting door to Ed's room briefly and smile hearing him moving round his room knowing he was going through much the same obsessive routine as me.

Having got out of the tac vest, it would be folded double and placed on the spare bed. The radio would be placed in its charger on my bedside table. My rifle would be wiped over, getting off any dust, the magazine taken off and the round in the breach ejected and the breach inspected for dirt. The magazine was replaced, and a round racked into the breach again, then the magazine taken off again, the round on the table loaded into the magazine and back on the rifle, safety on. If not fired recently, the rifle would be stripped and cleaned on my next day off. It would then be placed on the bed on top of the tac vest also in hands reach.

My pistol had the same treatment, except I would empty the magazine and reload a spare, allowing one of my five magazines to rest each day. Just a bit over the top? I often had that feeling. But remember, the threat level was through the roof, there was people out there that wanted us dead!

Having stripped off all my clothes and dropping them into a laundry basket to be collected by the cleaner, I'd lay out clean clothing on the spare bed ready for the evening shift, then collect up my duty belt and holster and step into the bathroom. At the Ebo Lele, there was a shower and a bath, therefore, so often after nights, I would relax in a hot bath for half an hour or so, clean my teeth and get into bed and check my e-mails, hopefully from the girls or the grandsons.

The curtains drawn, the air conditioning full blast, pistol under the pillow I would allow myself to drift off to sleep.

Did I put out the 'Do not disturb,' sign?

Bugger it!

1630hrs I was awake, then shaved, showered and refreshed, I dressed slowly in clean clothing, but didn't buff my boots, it was night duty, so no shiny surfaces. Others in the team would wear trainers, just as good, if not better, for creeping about the palace, but so often, following a tropical deluge, everything would be soddened with filthy water and ruin the trainers.

Nothing like spending the rest of your duty with stinking, wet feet.

1700hrs would see the three of us in the restaurant again and eating an early dinner, getting Camey to refill my flask with coffee and checking my day sack to make sure I had two bars of chocolate for the night.

Then off again to relieve the day team at the National Palace and do it all over again.

Our day off tomorrow, breakfast, some sleep and off to the El Rancho for a few hours relaxing in the sunshine then the Café de Latte for dinner.

What else?

Chapter 7

Just Another Day

I had got up at 0450 hours, the usual time for me to get myself out of bed, shaved and showered without rushing, and still have time to eat breakfast and have a cup of tea before the small team and I had to get to the National Palace and relieve the night team.

Normally, nights were quiet, and the team could kick back and every hour or so, send out a two man 'wandering patrol' through the palace and grounds waking up the palace guard force and rotate one of our men on the bridge covering the back of the president's apartments and overlooking most of the ground at the rear of the palace. Often, we would quietly walk up to the palace guards' sangers to find them asleep and so we would take their rifles and hide them nearby, wake them up and ask where their weapon was before handing it back to them. That alone would guarantee they remained awake for the rest of the night. No young guardsman wants to tell his superiors he cannot find his weapon. The occasions when there would be an evening reception, usually in the red saloon or some other event taking place elsewhere, would mean it was non-stop for whoever was on nights, and by 0700 hours, the whole team would be knackered and still facing the drive back to the Ibo Lele or our team house half way up Mountain Noir for sleep.

We had moved from Ebo Lele to the team house on Mountain Noir to give us better rooms and apart from breakfast, we would eat at the Café Fiore de Latte. This meant less chance of New Delhi belly especially after one of the team contacted typhoid, apparently caught from something in the kitchen

The drive to the National Palace would take about 30 minutes, assuming we were not troubled by roadblocks, such as trees dragged into the road, abandoned cars and burning tyres, occasionally just a tree branch. It took some understanding of the local culture to know what each, different obstruction meant or what it was saying. Occasionally, there were bodies, human bodies which we would have to drag aside to get our vehicle through. They were mostly men who had been either shot, and if it was an execution, the shot would be in the back of the head, usually making a mess at the front of the head. Very unpleasant, especially first thing in the morning. Or, they may have been stabbed to death, sometimes macheted, leaving the body very messy. These bodies are gruesome to see and horrific to deal with. But the most dreadful and disgusting murders were the poor people who had their lives ended by the 'Fiery Necklace'!

The 'Fiery Necklace' death is when a car's tyre inner rim is filled with petrol then hung round the victim's neck and set alight. Not an uncommon sight and that image would stay in your head for some time.

Today was just another day for me. Chris was on his day off and still in bed, if I remember correctly, Ed was at the National Palace, waiting for me to relieve him.

Just another sunny Haitian day.

I dressed, collected all the kit I might need for the day, dropped my previous day's sweaty clothing outside my room door to be washed and ironed by the two lovely local ladies who looked after us, as well as making our beds and cleaning our rooms. Then I would say, "Good Morning," to the big horrible, hairy spider that would come to the entrance of its hole opposite my room door in response to my footfall, stare at me for a few seconds with its front facing hunter's eyes, then return to its lair, and I would continue to make my way to the kitchen. That spider had really started to get to me. If it was not there waiting for me as I stepped from my room, I would find myself waiting for this creature of nightmares to appear. It made my skin creep. Either me or the spider will have to go. Of course, in the tropics there are spiders everywhere, waiting for you, in your bed, under your bed, in your clothing draws, everywhere. I was having breakfast at the Ibo Lele when a spider the size of my hand and outstretched fingers was spotted climbing a huge Palm Tree. Small birds were fluttering and squawking round it, the spider was after the young chicks in their nest at the top. It was chilling watching it climb slowly, silhouetted against the early morning sun. Our waiter, Camay, shook his head and tutted, "They kill my chickens," he said.

I shuddered.

I am naturally a morning person, and so having to be up and about at silly o'clock did not bother me as long as I had time for a proper cup of tea and a decent breakfast, so I opened and poured bottled water into the kettle to make that all important first cuppa of the day.

I had bought the teapot from the UK while on leave, and much to our American cousins' amusement, when demonstrating how real tea is made by the Brits, I would make a performance of it. Most of them had never seen or heard of a teapot before and did not quite grasp the importance of using boiling water, *"Not just hot water guys, boiling water."*

Howling laughter would, of course, usually accompany my demonstration. *"Hey guys, Marty is demonstrating how to make tea again. You don't wanna miss this."*

My American comrades only drank coffee as a beverage and then only black. Milk was only for wimps! There was a couple of real 'Beverley Hillbillies' among them, one proudly telling us Brits "My brother's in the Klan."

A real life 'Good ol' Boy.'

I had just finished stirring the pot when Brett, a South Londoner and former rifles sergeant walked into the kitchen. He had just finished a contract in Serbia and would tell us he needed the rest. So, a sunny Caribbean holiday in Haiti sounded just what he wanted.

"That's good timing, Brett." He also needed a decent cuppa to start his day off right.

He smiled and collected his mug from the draining board, returned to the table and sat opposite.

"Give it another couple of minutes before you pore," I said, wondering what to have for breakfast, which was the first important decision of the day I would make. Usually, it was either cereal of some sort or scrambled eggs and plenty of toast, trying to alternate between the two as the eggs would not last me long, as they were so small. I would call them 'Third World' eggs, as it took at least 6 of them to make half decent scrambled eggs on toast.

Now you may ask, what am I going on about? Third World eggs and cereals? But when you are facing an uncertain twelve-hour day, and not really knowing when, or if, you may be able to get another meal inside you, then little matters such as eggs, toast or Rice Crispies for breaky take on a whole new meaning to your day. This food, together with a couple of cups of tea, that's builders' tea bought back in the UK, and one is then ready for anything the day may throw at you.

This was going to be one of those days.

Brett poured out the tea into our personalised mugs. I believe mine had "Big Bastard" printed on it. Both our radios suddenly crackled, as if someone was pressing the 'speak' button. This was most extraordinary, as no one ever spoke over the net between midnight and 0700, unless there was an emergency.

No message came through and we assumed someone had accidentally pressed the button. We continued drinking tea, our noses deep inside the mugs, with me still wondering what to have for breakfast.

As I have mentioned previously, we all carried a lot of gear when on duty, and so, apart from the kit I would carry on my duty belt, pistol, spare mags, Asp, knife and radio, there was my tac vest (tactical vest), its pockets filled with M16 magazines, personal trauma kit, mobile phone, notebook and pen, and just about anything else I could think of.

The tac vest was heavy when I was not actually wearing the thing, and so it was carried in a canvas holdall. My primary weapon was the M16 rifle from the Vietnam era, and a very user-friendly weapon compared to other weapon systems I have found myself using in other places, and finally I had a secondary weapon, a semi-automatic shotgun. The Benelli is an awesome beast. On the firing range, I could fire off all seven rounds before the first cartridge case would hit the ground. The ideal weapon then, for breaching doors, that is, blowing off the hinges, then kicking down the door: devastating at close combat.

The problem was all the extra ammunition I would have to carry for this weapon as well. It all went into the canvas holdall, and it was heavy.

Brett had a similar amount of equipment to lug about with him but sitting down that morning drinking our tea he mused, "I don't think I'll take my tac vest today."

He sounded as if he was speaking to himself: daydreaming really.

I remember replying, interrupting his reverie, "It's sod's law mate. If you don't take it, you're going to need it."

"It's so bloody heavy," he complained.

"So is running out of ammo," I countered.

"Yeah," he grumbled and took another sip of tea. I had decided to have scrambled eggs on toast for breakfast, as our radios crackled into life.

"The Palace is surround by burning tyres and smoke. There is in-coming gunfire. We need the 'rapid response' here now!"

It was Oz, the American night commander at the National Palace. His voice was calm but with an urgent edge. I could hear the rattle of gunfire over our radios.

Brett and I looked at each other wide eyed for a couple of seconds taking in this message. Then Brett stood and said, "I'll get my tac vest." I began to get into mine.

Oz continued to give a running commentary on the events unfolding before him saying the others of the team had deployed around the top floor of the palace where President Aristide's apartments were.

But they were very thin on the ground. He needed us there now!

The voice of Gale, the day's detail leader, called over the radio, "Break, Break!" radio speak for everyone to clear the net. He continued, "All Steele units to RV at Plas Boyer," a square some hundred metres from the Iron Bridge, a prearranged rendezvous between the various places the whole team lived. The first units arriving there would secure the area and wait for the others.

Brett arrived back at the kitchen still struggling into his tac vest said grinning, "It's still bloody heavy."

I had just zipped up mine, shrugging to make it sit more comfortably when Chris suddenly appeared wearing only his underpants, looking sleepy and dishevelled, rubbing his head clearly confused, asking, "What's going on?"

"Chris," I said, chuckling at his appearance. "Get some socks on. It sounds like the 'White House' is under attack. We're moving in two minutes!"

Without a word, Chris turned and ran back to his room.

I had always admired Chris at times like this. It takes an awful lot of moral fibre, not to mention cold-blooded courage, to face the dangerous unknown when suddenly woken up from a sleep. The natural impulse is to dive under the bed, surely? It is times like this when you find out who's up for it and who's not! Chris always was, whatever and wherever the dangers where we faced.

I had the car started as Brett got in and sat next to me, Chris still dressing with equipment and firearms dangling from his arms and clothing round his neck dived into the back of the vehicle.

"Where we going?" he asked.

"Meeting the others at the Plas Boyer RV," I replied and honked the horn for our Haitian night watchman to open the gate.

Surprisingly, the night watchman was already waiting for us.

"*Umm curious,*" and it's these seemingly unimportant little curiosities, something small, going almost un-noticed and outside the perceived norm, so easy to overlook that gets you killed in my world.

After all, we were leaving the residence almost an hour earlier that morning and would normally have to wake him. But as 'They' say in Haiti, "It's all *smoke and mirrors.*" Only believe half of what you see, and nothing of what you hear." He knew something was up though, probably told by the drums that on some nights would be ceaseless. There was always something disturbing about the night in Haiti.

If I were asked to describe Haiti in one sentence it would be; 'Gunshots, screams and drums in the night.'

Haiti has something of the dark continent in everything that went on, especially in the hours of darkness: something darkly spiritual and foreboding.

In the quiet, creepy small hours of the mist-shrouded night, when I was patrolling the forty acres of the president's private residence's plantation, sudden wailing screams would shatter the stillness, and I would then find myself retracing my steps and revisiting all the isolated guard posts on the plantation to reassure and settle the fearful Haitian guard force.

Voodoo!

Well, here in Western Europe, it is something we might laugh at or be entertained by, but in Haiti, it is a part of their everyday life, something the people really do live and breathe, a religion. It is closely aligned to the Roman Catholic Church rituals, certainly, no one laughs at it, as it pervades every corner of Haitian society, shedding darkness where there should be light. There is something very real and tangible about it, you could feel it constantly, especially in the hours of darkness. It's something you could almost touch, if not for the *smoke and mirrors*.

At the bottom of the Ibo Lele hill, there is a right turn into a narrow lane leading to crossroads. To the left is the Iron Bridge where Chris and I had our deadly confrontation with three rogue Haitian Police Officers. To the right is another residential road and straight on, is Plas Boyer and our RV point.

I had always a bad feeling when turning into that narrow lane, knowing that combined with the crossroads just a few yards on, it was an ideal ambush point. Indeed, if I wanted to ambush the likes of us, then that is exactly where I would have placed it. I had mentioned this to our American colleagues, but they shrugged saying, "We'll take it as it comes, partner."

Silly sods!

Still, there were some others who felt the same, certainly Ed and Brett. Chris would just duck every time we drove through the lane and out across the junction. So that morning, obeying the warning voice speaking quietly in my head, we stopped at the narrow lane, dismounted and cleared and secured the lane and crossroads. Then continued to the RV.

What better then to lure us out by faking an attack on the National Palace and ambush us at these crossroads? From the Ibo Lele and our team house on Mountain Noir, there was no other route to the palace. We had to cross that killing ground and I could easily imagine automatic weapons opening-up on us from two positions at the junction and a 'choke' in the narrow lane behind us, preventing any retreat. It was a perfect killing ground, but not that morning. But I still shuddered when I finally drove our vehicle across that junction. As I have said, it is not easy being brave when just out of bed that early in the morning.

Our little team were the first to arrive at the RV. We secured the square, took cover in the dark gloom and waited for the others to arrive. Plas Boyer is in Petionville, a relatively well-off neighbourhood, especially compared with the poorer parts of Port au Prince, although the housing was modest and careworn. But the first thing you would notice was each house was surrounded by a high wall, mostly with barbed wire on top and an iron panelled gate, and that the guard dogs had begun to bark.

Our American colleagues were only a few minutes behind, arriving with the usual noise and slamming of car doors.

"Morning Marty." Marty always grated on me, but it was their way. They were a very friendly bunch but from a different culture: two nations divided by a common language.

"We cleared the lane and crossroads. That's why we're a mite late."

"Okay, what's the plan?" I asked, smiling inwardly to myself.

"Let's get to the palace and punch through anything that gets in our way!"

"Right," I said.

"Right!" I thought, *"Here we go."* There is nothing like a good plan.

"Mount up!" Gale shouted. He was the most switched-on former GI there. But I think he must have been in the US Marine Naval Cavalry or some such non-existent unit, as he was forever using terms such as "Attention on deck!" and "Mount up!" I liked Gale, as did most of the Brits.

And so, I found myself driving the lead vehicle with Gale, Chris and Brett.

Canopy Verde is the main road and the most direct route into the centre of Port au Prince and the

National Palace, and we made good time, until the road narrowed and was blocked by smoking burnt out cars and piles of burning tyres. This roadblock was at the start of a hill between shanties on our left and the local brothel to our right. We knew it was a brothel, it had a grimy red-light bulb glowing faintly in the darkness, hanging by a thin thread of wire.

The shanties were on the side of a hill and terraced down to the edge of the roadway. The brothel on our right was edging the road but the land dropped away behind with more terraced shanties into a ravine, more than enough cover for 'Them' to ambush us, there and then.

I stopped the vehicle some twenty-five yards from the barrier and gave cover with Gale, me with my shotgun and Gale with his MP5, as Brett and Chris moved forward to the roadblock, taking cover behind the smouldering vehicles, their Uzi sub machine guns raised ready to return fire.

There was silence, not a sound. Everything was still, and we braced ourselves for an attack. I sensed "They" were close and watching us. I could feel dozens of pairs of eyes watching me from cover, and asked myself *"Was it our night-watchman who told "Them" we were on our way?"* Were "They" in the shanties or hiding in the darkness? The place was creepy, and I prepared myself for whatever was to happen next.

A hail of stones and other debris showered down on us from an unknown location. It was almost dawn, and I couldn't tell where the stuff was coming from, I was not even sure if it came from our right or left. That of course, adds another dimension to the threat facing you and adds to your uncertainty and fear. The need to keep a tight control on yourself is now important, as the desire to fire off a couple of hundred rounds into the shanties was very real. The atmosphere was very threatening and frightening in that misty dawn, the only real light coming from the guttering fires at the roadblock.

I felt a light touch on my shoulder. It was Gale.

"Marty, fire off a couple of rounds and let's see what happens."

Gale stepped away from me as I fired two rounds from the shotgun into the air.

The crash of my gunfire split the dawn silence and echoed back from the bottom of the ravine. It was followed by the same eerie silence and stillness, a silence you felt you could touch. There were people in those shanties, but they remained silent and I imagined mothers holding their children tight to them, stopping them from crying out in terror. We were all frightened that morning and I could hear gunfire coming from the direction of the National Palace.

"Okay, let's go forward and make a hole in the barrier," Gale said, in a low voice, as in deference to the dawn's menacing air.

He touched my shoulder again, "Marty, stay here, use that," he nodded at the shotgun in my hands, "Only if you have to, then make it count. No prisoners, we have to get to the palace asap." He looked in the direction of the palace briefly listening to the gunfire, then went forward to the barrier.

Another vehicle with others of our unit had arrived and together they shifted a burnt-out car to make a gap to get our vehicles through. Chris facing up at the shanties to our left and Brett facing down past the brothel at the other shanties as they dropped away down the ravine, while I covered our rear.

I heard Gale call quietly again, "Mount up," and we ran to our vehicles and drove through the gap in the barrier onward to the centre of Port au Prince.

The relief in our vehicle as we drove on to the National Palace was palpable, it had been a very tense few minutes. How long had it been? Just a few minutes? As usual, I would find that time had stood still, or rather I had lost track of time. Was it just a few minutes or was it hours?

It is times like this when you are committed to doing whatever is necessary to complete your mission and then be thankful afterwards there had been no violence and you hadn't had to injure or kill. I well remember a time when I was driving the chase vehicle in one of the president's motorcades. The chase vehicle was a big four-wheel drive land-cruiser driven by an experienced chase driver. The team leader sat next to the driver and two others in the back, automatic weapons up and pointing out of the rear windows screening the president's vehicle on his left side ready to give covering fire should the motorcade come under attack. Our Haitian counterparts were in a similar vehicle screening the right side of the president's vehicle.

On narrow roads, our two vehicles would travel line abreast behind the president, and it was then you were reminded very starkly of your own vulnerability. For our counterparts would have their automatic weapons pointed out of their rear windows, and of course pointed at us in the other chase vehicle, their triggers fingers on their individual triggers. I would imagine what could happen if their vehicle hit a bump! We were forever telling them to keep their trigger finger outside the trigger guard. It never stuck, and I remember another guard force in another part of the world having the same problem with their trigger fingers, and so I witnessed one of those guards, a young lad shoot himself in the foot. Not once, but twice, with a large calibre semi-automatic weapon.

On another occasion, when I was chase driver, Chris leaned forward from the rear gunner's seat and said, "There's a motorbike in the motorcade coming up fast!"

"Oh great!" I thought and saw in my side mirror a motorbike coming up fast on my inside. Ed, who was in the team leader's seat that day said tersely, "Take him out Martyn, if the others don't get him first!"

A motorbike is the classic assassin's transport for getting themselves to a moving target, and then getting themselves away after their attack. I decreased speed allowing him to approach quicker and mentally committed myself to certainly killing this rider with a sideswipe that would plunge the rider at speed into the unforgiving bottom of the ditch, it looked some 10 feet deep.

The motorbike came to within feet of the rear of my vehicle when Chris leaned forward and urgently said, "It's alright, he's HNP (meaning Haitian National Police.) probably arrived late for the motorcade!" HNP always has two outriders in front of the president's motorcades.

"Jesus!" I remember shouting in relief. I really had not wanted to kill anyone that day if it could be avoided. That HNP outrider would never know how lucky he was, and thanks especially to Chris who recognised what he was.

Think of it, arrive late for work, do your best to catch up on your work and get killed for the trouble. One man, me, about to snatch his life, and Chris a man he did not know, never even heard of, who had saved his life. All taking place in a fleeting moment, in one of the chase vehicles and him totally unaware of this drama. How tenuous life was in my world.

I felt the light touch of Chris hand on my shoulder. We would talk about this incident at dinner later that evening. He knew how I felt.

Johnny Cash fans will recall his hit record *Ring of fire*. Well following the negotiation of the burning barrier, we found ourselves singing, "We drove into a burning ring of tyres." I can't recall who started the singing, probably Brett. He was a bit of a muso. It certainly eased the tension and plucked our courage up. We still had to get to the National Palace and deal with whatever was waiting for us there.

The remainder of the drive to the palace was uneventful save for the eerie stillness, no one on the streets, no cars on the roads. Usually the centre of Port au Prince would be teeming with people and traffic, all going about their daily lives. Street sellers hawking matches, candles, drinks and other simple basic everyday items. Not cigarettes though, the poor had no money for cigarettes, some not even knowing where the next mouthful of food was coming from.

But today, the streets were empty, the pavements bare of vendors, not even street children who would run beside moving vehicles with beaming smiles on their happy faces, hands out asking for money. Especially the Blancs. The street children knew we were soft touches.

Our vehicles burst out from a side street onto the National Palace square, a large area bounded by a formal square to the front of the palace and a large park to one side. The other sides were edged with government buildings and if I recall correctly, the tomb of Dessalines himself, one of Haiti's leaders during the 1802 revolution and a later Governor-General.

The square was shrouded with smoke from burning tyres, gunfire all round us, so much we could not tell precisely the direction it was coming from. The gunmen were shooting from the cover of the government buildings, and still firing at the palace. They had not seen us yet, possibly the smoke was in our favour for a change.

Gale shouted over the radios, "Sierra! Sierra!" our radio-speak meaning the South Gate, the main gate at the back of the palace, hopefully to confuse any of the opposition listening in on our frequency.

I accelerated down the side of the Palace the park to my left, turned right onto the road running down the rear, housing the barracks and parade ground of the palace guard force, brass band and SWAT Team.

I was lead vehicle and driving at speed, the other vehicles close behind. Chris, Brett and Gale with their weapons up and out of the windows. No prisoners here either.

Chris shouted, "Hope they have the gate open," voicing what we were all thinking.

At least I was driving and had something to keep my mind off the fear of what might be waiting for us. My three comrades were alone with their fears.

Fear is a lonely place.

"Open or not, I'm driving through!" I replied and looked up at the rear-view mirror and saw Chris, a look of grim determination on his face.

Nobody had fired at us, but it was only a matter of time before "They" realised who we were and got their act together.

I turned sharp right into the open gates of the South Entrance of the National Palace. Yes, remarkably, the gates were open.

I shouted to Chris and Brett "Watch this lot! Don't trust anyone here!" and swept through the portal and onto the parade ground, our other vehicles following close behind.

Dozens of palace guards and bandsmen were milling about leaderless and clearly unsure what was expected of them. But the obvious relief on their faces when seeing us Blancs was reassuring, as it probably meant they were on our side, for the time being anyway. The palace guards and bandsmen were not combat troops, not trained with weapons, the guards had rifles that they had probably never fired and almost certainly did not have more than a few rounds of ammunition anyway. The SWAT team was a different matter, well-armed and trained by the Blancs' training team. Where were they? Hopefully, deployed round the palace perimeter. The problem was there were not enough of them to make a difference defending the palace against a large organised attacking force. We still had no idea who "They" were and how many of "Them" there were. It was only the chickens that morning that looked relaxed and calm as they continued their usual wandering and scratching round the palace grounds.

"Marty, cover the back. I need eyes here. Get those gates shut and kick arse!" Gale shouted at the others to follow him and ran towards the rear staircase of the Palace leading to the presidential residence and offices.

I turned and ran to the gate shouting at the confused and frightened guards, "Firme la port!" and reaching the gate, grabbed one of the huge doors and began to swing it shut. The guards jumped into life and helped. Then grabbing any guards with stripes on their uniform sleeves, I told them firmly in the universal language of sign and obscenities to stay at this gate and not open it for anyone. Their smiles and nods of agreement told me they had understood, happy now that they had been given orders, no more uncertainty.

I returned to the parade ground and saw some SWAT running towards the South West guard post, a large and roofed concreted sanger in this isolated part of the palace grounds.

This South West sanger was positioned next to the former prison, now derelict, but once used by Papa Doc Duvalier and his Ton Ton Macoot thugs to interrogate, torture and murder their victims. There was a dreadful atmosphere hanging over the place. I had once stepped inside but was unable to go deeper into the building as the structure appeared about to collapse, but also there was a strong negative presence that told me I was not welcome. I backed out never to enter the place again.

However, it was this sanger that was sited in this remote part of the palace grounds I visited regularly on my patrols either early in the mornings or late at night, invariably having to wake up the guards.

I followed the SWAT, needing to know what was going on there. As I rounded the corner, the SWAT were kneeling behind a low wall returning fire to gunmen that had probed this side of the grounds. Rounds were cracking and clapping about me and I quickly decided to gain the apparent safety of the sanger.

Wrong move!

The sanger was taking fire. The guard in there was sitting on the concrete floor, his back to the wall under the sanger's window looking at me wide-eyed in terror. This man had been completely unnerved by the attack and was rigid with fear and had been on his own during the attack and had now only just been re-enforced with the SWAT and me. I could not blame him as the rounds were coming through the opening above his head and ricocheting off the walls and buzzing like angry wasps all over the place. His rifle was lying a few feet away from him. It appeared to have been discarded, an action not uncommon with those that no longer have the taste to carry on. He was out of the fight! Being alone when in mortal danger is a place no one should ever be. You draw courage and strength from your comrades at times like this. I would have to keep an eye on this position.

I shouted to no one, "Oh shit!" and threw myself back out of the sanger and landed in the dust and chicken shit, but otherwise unharmed and joined the SWAT, a few yards away at the wall. It was safer!

My radio squawked, "Sparrow? Stallion, over." It was Gale.

I answered, "Sparrow."

"Sparrow, I hear gunfire coming from your sector. How you doing there? Stallion over."

"Sierra Whisky sanger taking fire. SWAT at my location and returning fire. Sparrow Over."

"Marty!" Gale had used open language usually reserved for extreme moments in radio speak. "If it looks like you are to be overrun, you high-tail it out of there and fall back on us. You hear me? How copy? Over."

"Roger that!" I replied, only too happy to know I had the all clear to run like hell when and if that time came.

I looked to where the firing was coming from. There were certainly numerous gunmen shooting at us, but they did not seem to want to cross the open ground and probe deeper into the Palace grounds. That is the problem when in a firefight, you find what you feel is a safe and comfortable place to shoot from and are unwilling to leave your safe place and expose yourself while taking more ground.

My thoughts at this time were to let them use their ammunition and I'll use mine when I have clear targets. I motioned to the SWAT to hold their fire and shoot only at clear targets. They loved to just blast away with no real targets sighted.

My thoughts drifted to Ed and Chris, wondering how they were getting on, I could hear gunfire coming from their position. Then my thoughts were with my family at home and I quickly shook these thoughts out of my mind, I had a job to get on with. Too late for second thoughts, and I was being paid very well for this lark.

Gradually, the attackers fire began to slow, they had realised that they were running low on ammunition, and more importantly, it dawned on them that, as we were behind the wall, we were not going anywhere. I stepped back over to the sanger, the guard was still sat on the floor his head now drooped and he looked up as I crouched in the doorway. "Packy problem?" I asked gently. He shook his head wearily, raised a hand and replied, "Packy problem." I gave him the thumbs-up and ran over to the South Gate again. It was still closed, and the guards stared at me for reassurance. I smiled and gave them the thumbs-up as well and their faces lit up in bright smiles of relief. I had to remind them to keep the gate closed until told otherwise. Their attention span was somewhat erratic.

I returned to the South West sanger; the incoming fire had almost ceased. The opposition were still taking pot-shots at us crouching behind the low wall. Nothing accurate, but we still needed to keep our heads down.

A few more SWAT arrived, grinning at me as they took up positions alongside their comrades. I gingerly stepped back inside the sanger and took a good look across the junction towards the opposition's positions. There was nothing to be seen, as they were well hidden inside the buildings. That was the thing about Aristide's murderous opposition, nobody really knew who 'They' were, apart from the disaffected mulatto establishment and only when spoken of always were referred to as 'Them' or, 'They'. We were forever being told "They are coming tonight, be ready!" We would ask, "Who are they?" The informer would shrug their shoulders and reply "Them." No one knew, but today was demonstrating "They" were a real and tangible threat.

"Marty?" I startled as my radio came to life.

"Marty," I answered. It was Gale.

"Gimme a sit-rep. Over."

"Very little incoming now. Believe 'They' are running low on ammo. I have more SWAT at my location. Over." I looked over at the men from SWAT. They were looking more relaxed.

"Yeah, that's the same here. Marty, I want you to check the West Gate, just to let the guards know we haven't forgotten them, and the East Sanger. Then fall back on my location. How copy? Over."

"Copy that." I glanced at my watch; it was 1540. I had been here at the southern part of the National Palace since well before 0800. Eight hours had passed. I looked at my watch again not trusting my first look. Sure enough it was 1540 hours. The past eight hours felt more like ten minutes and I continued my message to Gale. "Your order timed at 1540 hours."

"Copy that Marty. Gale out." I did not want anyone later to ask why I had left my post. Gale knew what I was on about.

I gave my SWAT companions the thumbs up and they returned the salute with grins and "Packy problem!" Then I ran over to the South Gate and did the same there. This time the guards, all of them grinning replied in unison "Packy problem!" No problem! The attack appeared to be over this side of the palace.

Running past the back of the garrison kitchens, I held my breath as always; the stench of rotting food was overpowering, and I climbed the few steps into the East Sanger. The guard and a couple of SWATs were relaxing and another guard dozing in the bright afternoon sunshine. "All okay here then," I thought. "Packy problem?" I asked.

"Packy problem," they replied. Well those who were awake anyway.

I took a deep breath and ran back past the kitchens again, past the inner gate leading to the palace itself and waved at my two comrades manning the bridge joining the red saloon and the presidential apartments on the second floor. It was high and anyone there had an excellent view of the inner gate, the parade ground and the South Gate beyond. I had been comforted by their presence, knowing I would have covering fire if my position had become untenable and I was retreating for dear life.

They waved back shouting, "Where have you been? Overslept?"

"Yeah. But you can relax now, I'm here."

I got the finger for that one.

The West Gate was as quiet as the East Sanger, the guards alert and nervous, and very pleased to see me and know they had not been forgotten in all the excitement by the Blancs. I stayed with them for a few minutes, but the gunfire had stopped, and the smoke was beginning to clear, as I ran back to the rear of the palace past the small and battered plaque to Papa Doc Duvalier for dedicating a drinking trough to the workers at the palace some thirty or so years previously. Then through the inner gate and up the steps into the palace and my comrades, much to the playful jeers and laughter of the two on the walkway above.

"Better late than never," was ringing in my ears.

The rest of the presidential protection unit were all outside the red saloon at the balcony windows overlooking the lawn at the front of the palace and the palace Square beyond. There were perhaps, hundreds of spent cartridge cases lying all over the marble flooring.

I spotted Ed and Chris, we made eye contact, acknowledging each other.

"Marty," Gale greeted me. "Get yourself coffee and whatever's in the fridge. It won't be a lot."

Brett called over, "Pop out and get us all pizzas mate." He was fiddling with his tac vest.

I sat in the CP sipping coffee, there was nothing left to eat in the fridge, but I was not hungry. I had not been hungry all day, perhaps too much other stuff going on. The others began drifting in, the firing had stopped and there was movement around the palace again.

Gale appeared, calling, "Attention on deck!" and behind him walked the president and Madame Aristide. The president was smiling and looking dapper in his white suit as always, while the first lady was looking tired and drawn. We all stood to attention, but the president waved us down as Madame Aristide said, "Oh no, please sit."

President Aristide looked us over, thinking about what he was to say.

"On behalf of myself, my family and of course my government, I would like to thank each and every one of you for your courage and steadfastness during the day. We would not be here now if not for your support." The first lady stood next to him, smiling her agreement.

When they had left the CP, I sat and finished the remains of my coffee, suddenly feeling exhausted. Chris was on his lap-top, Brett was dozing, and Ed was chatting to Gale. How quickly everything returns to normal, even after a day such as this one had been, and I was beginning to feel very hungry.

Moments later, the cook and her assistant came into the CP with bottles of Coca Cola, bowls of salad, boiled eggs and bread.

Ooh Ahh! I was ready for this and my mouth was watering.

I knew the salad would end up giving me the New Delhi belly and the coke would repeat on me, but I was too hungry and too tired by then to care and tucked in, finding a chair next to Ed and Chris. It was nice to have their company again as so often and especially on this contract, I would find myself wondering if I would ever see my two friends again.

Later, I walked over to one of the huge Georgian windows that looked out over the front lawn of the palace and the main square of Port au Prince beyond. Immediately, I was knocked backwards, mentally overwhelmed by the terrifying sight evolving before me, wide eyed in awe and dread.

There was easily ten thousand people running into the square towards the palace from the direction of Bel Air, a chaotic and crumbling mass of insanitary tenement housing and shanties.

"We're going to need more ammo!" I called to the others. "There's a small manifestation out there!" Manifestation is a Haitian term for a gathering or crowd of people. We always laughed at the term, but not this time.

My companions rushed to the windows, and then turned and began grabbing their weapons, concern on their faces. It had not finished.

Gale called, his voice shaky, "Top floor, top of the staircases, we'll defend from there, Marty…."

He paused, looking at the gathering mob. I thought, rolling my eyes, *"What now, can I have Chris or Ed with me this time? Not another 8 hours dodging bullets on my own!"*

Gale continued, "They don't look hostile…"

The CP door opened, and a laughing palace guard shouted, "Packy problem" and left to join the celebrations.

One of the president's Haitian Secret Service arrived, grinning all over his handsome face and assured us it was over. I hadn't seen any of our Haitian counterparts during the assault on the palace.

"Umm."

We relaxed, flopping into whatever chair was closest, it was a demonstration of support by the president's grass roots followers.

Hurrah!

The thought, however, did not escape me, *"So I get to live another day…."*

Gale was standing next to me lighting a cigarette, gazing out of the window and I noticed his hands were shaking. I looked away, not wanting him to see I had noticed. It had been that sort of day and this last alarm had just about done us all in, physically and mentally. I think now I hadn't any fight left in me, I just wanted to go to bed.

Later Gale said, "Marty, Chris, Brett stand down. Get some sleep and be here for 0700 tomorrow. Sorry about your day off, Chris.' That brought a smile to our faces, we grabbed our gear for the journey back to the team house. We would travel in convey with Ed and others of the team. The gunfire had stopped but the danger was not over. It never was in Haiti. Besides, it was now dark out there!

I looked at my watch again, it was 2000 hours. I was tired and wanted a shower and just flop into bed.

"You ready?" I called to Chris adding to Brett, "Don't forget your tac vest mate." Our eyes met, and we exchanged knowing looks, and I realising for the first time that day I had missed breakfast.

The most important meal of the day! When you have time, that is.

Back at the team house, I collected my holdall bag from the car's boot. I had fired off dozens of rounds during my eight hours at the rear of the palace, but the bag was still bloody heavy.

"Where's my bed!"

The spider was waiting for me at the entrance of its lair. I returned its stare. It did not frighten me; I had used up all my fear for the day at the National Palace. The spider returned down its hole, and I like to think it sulked. I opened the door to my room and stepped inside as the drums began to beat.

My sanctuary was cool, the light dim and shadowy as I dropped the holdall and tac vest where I stood, placed both shotgun and rifle on my bed, took my pistol from its holster on the tac vest and stuffed it into the holster on my duty belt. Then, stepping into the bathroom, hung the belt on a clothes hook, the pistol still in hands reach, stripped off my clothing letting it all drop round my feet, and stepped into the shower.

Bliss!

Chapter 8

Café Fiore de Latte

This charming oasis is where Ed, Chris and I would often lunch together when our days off coincided. It was opposite the St Pierre Bar, where the guys would gather in the evenings for a couple of beers. On the corner of the road opposite, which lead down to the flower market, there was an ever-expanding pothole. It had been noticeably increasing in circumference and depth in my time in Haiti but had clearly been growing for years. Now, writing of pot holes, I remember driving in a motorcade down another road and vehicles in front swerving for no apparent reason and Gale shouting to me in the excitement and tension of the speeding convoy, "They're driving round a pot hole that's not there anymore, it was filled in ages ago!" So, some time ago, there was a pothole that had, months previously, had been filled in, but local drivers who had been using this stretch of road forever, including our motorcade drivers, still swerved to miss this now phantom pothole.

Smoke and mirrors?

But the pothole opposite the Fiore de Latte was mega enormous and if anyone had fallen into it, they would have either drowned, for it was usually filled with rainwater, or died from exposure and starvation as they would never have climbed out.

This area was controlled by Nickson and his second in command Jackson, who ran the local prostitutes, known as Coco Rats by our American colleagues, and Bouzen by the locals. The Americans had the term Coco Rats wrong, as Coco is Haitian slang for a vagina and Rats were the men who used them. Street urchins would beg and steal, sell Nickson's drugs, keep an eye on the prostitutes and act as lookouts for any intruder on Nickson's turf, known as 'maximum security', an accurate descriptive name, as the weapons they carried were serious. They carried machine pistols on them and pump action shotguns waiting in their car for drive-by shootings or street beefs as other gangs would probe their patch, regularly snatching their prostitutes and killing any street urchin that got in their way. When we visited the St Pierre Bar and Grill or the Fiore de Latte, we would always flip one of the boys a few dollars. We never had any problems in that part of town and our vehicles were never touched.

The Café Fiore de Latte was owned and managed by a lovely Swiss lady whose husband, a banker, managed one of the international banks in Port au Prince. I cannot recall their names, but she did tell me that some twenty years previously in London, she had been an au pair for the children of a husband and wife, both Labour members of Parliament and junior ministers.

What a small world we all live in.

The restaurant was a smart, quiet oasis surrounded by a high thick hedge that wrapped round the gardens. The clientele were very upper middle-class Haitians and ex-pats from the diplomatic corps of a dozen countries who would bring their children at lunchtimes. It was an enchanting, romantic place to be in the evenings. The children would be able to enjoy a huge selection of ice creams designed to keep them quiet for a while, so mothers could chat with each other. The owner's salads were to die for, especially after she told me all the ingredients were thoroughly washed in bottled water before being served. The menu was small, but her dishes really did melt in one's mouth. She was not the Chef; he was a French Canadian and there were a lot of other French Canadians either owning or working in restaurants who were wonderful chefs. We even met France, a very attractive French-Canadian lady, who owned and ran a casino in Port au Prince. How can I put it; she would have needed a powerful personality with powerful connections to be able to operate a casino in Port au Prince. Most restaurants, nightclubs and bars had overtly armed guards on their doors, the firearm usually being a pump action shotgun. But not the Café Fiore de Latte, as any customers from the diplomatic corps or their families would have had security either outside in vehicles, or seated at other tables nearby, so any threat there would be over with a dozen of us drawing weapons at one time. I never did have the New Delhi belly from eating there.

Just sitting there in the daytime, having their wonderful coffee, was magical, as the gardens were lush with beautiful tropical plants and flowers and stunning orchids. Add to this scene, hummingbirds flitting from flower to Orchid at shoulder height, as we sat at our table.

There, we would recognise American Airlines cabin staff we had met on the flight from Miami and they would tell us about trying to train fearful young Haitian girls to be cabin crew, who, on take-offs and landings, would sit in the cabin crew seats opposite the now concerned passengers, fingering their rosaries tearfully.

Following our lunch, we would visit the El Rancho hotel, made famous by Graham Greene in his novel *The Comedians*, later made into a major Hollywood film, starring Richard Burton and Elizabeth Taylor, Peter Ustinov, and Alec Guinness, all "A" list film stars of their day. There, we would spend the rest of our day off, lounging by the pool, Chris relaxing and drinking rum punches, not Ed or I though, we were tea-total and would look down our noses playfully at Chris. It never stopped him from enjoying those rum punches.

I really wanted to try one, but not in front of Ed!

Chapter 9

Cactus

The Plantation, or the Forty Acres, code name Cactus, the indefensible family home of the President of the Republic of Haiti gave me pause for thought when I became familiar with its size and layout. Most of the estate was, as one of its names implies, mature banana, pineapples plants, hardwoods such as the huge mango trees and palms. Together with other tropical vegetation, this gave it the jungle effect that stretched from just behind the house gardens and swimming pool down to the isolated high back wall of the property and the two sangers at each end of that wall, some two hundred metres apart. For the two lone guards, especially at night in the dark, it was a frightening place and should an organised force execute even a simple frontal attack, these guards would, of course, have taken to their heels leaving only us, the presidential protection unit there at the time, to fall back on the house with the three of us likely to die there.

Any support from our counterparts did not enters our heads. Not a pleasant thought, for any possible re-enforcement would be, like the palace, at least an hour away.

So as at the palace, it was prudent to be proactive in patrolling and talking to the guard force, knowing they would be aware of any heightened threat before us with ourselves sensing the reason for their nervousness when visiting the sangers.

The journey from Mountain Noir was about the same length of time as getting to the National Palace and of course, at night, in the dark, it was 'guns up!' all the way through the vegetable market on our left, then the fuel garage, also on the left of us. These waypoints helped us measure the distance travelled from the Ebo Lele, for Ed, Chris and me, now the team house on Mountain Noir.

The halfway marker to the plantation was the open fronted mortuary on our right. Melting slabs of ice with, what we presumed were bodies wrapped in white sheeting, lay on them as the melt ran into and across the road, forming deep everlasting puddles in the potholes. But the most alarming location on our journey to Cactus was another mile or so from the mortuary at a crossroads where three roads came together at a junction where a now derelict police post and barrier had stood guarding the roads. For in the middle of this junction was a steel re-enforcing rod that projected at an angle of some forty-five degrees from the tarmac, waiting to rip out an engine from a vehicle or tear off its wheels should the driver be unaware of this hazard. It had been there for years. It was there throughout my time in Haiti and probably still there now.

Or perhaps the dreadful earthquake fixed the problem?

Another two miles or so on and to our right, were the main gates of Cactus. Two large, high, wrought iron gates that certainly would not have been a problem for a heavy lorry. This popular means of dynamic attack that would smash through and with no heavy machine gun to support this gate, the lorry would race for the inner gate leaving rebels on foot to mop up any remaining guards at the main gate. Within seconds, we would have been fighting for our lives and the lives of the president and family.

Did I say I liked nights at Cactus?

The inner gate allowed access to the residence's front garden turning circle where we would line up the motorcade when the president and family would return to the palace. Always, the two identical presidential vehicles would wait at the bottom of the steps outside the front door where, if I were not driving the chase vehicle, I would stand waiting on 'maximum standby' and watch the hummingbirds just a few feet away, flittering from orchid to orchid hanging from the trees at the front of the house. On these same steps on late warm summer evenings, the president and first lady would be sat and acknowledge my formal greeting as I passed and made my way towards the door almost hidden by ivy in the back-garden wall. I would step out into the jungle, take a few steps into the foliage then crouch and wait, sometimes for up to fifteen minutes, to allow my eyes to adjust to the darkness.

To the right of the main house was located our CP which we shared with our counterparts although in two separate parts of the single storied building. Our counterparts had a small office and another room with bunk beds which we envied, for our room was small with a desk and four uncomfortable chairs facing a bank of CCTV screens showing black and white pictures of the gates and various other locations of the rear gardens that also backed onto an outside wall. On stormy nights, the images on screen would have a real and spooky film noir look leaving us with little enthusiasm to leave the CP.

But the chairs were too small for me to relax in and at best, only allowed a fitful doze, so I would volunteer for first watch in the president's rear garden in the comfortable garden chair under the mango tree and just a couple of metres from his kitchen door. There, my head wrapped in a towel protecting me from the mosquitoes, I would spend the first couple of hours of the night and later, in the last hours before dawn at the end of our shift at Cactus, I would unwrap from my day sack a beach towel and drape it round my shoulders against the chill.

Late in the evening, I would be relieved by either Ed or Chris and return to the CP, passing the room where our counterparts would be snoring away and into our room and a chocolate bar and coffee, feet up on the desk and prepare myself physically and mentally for my wandering patrol through the jungle and rest of the estate.

I did not want anything on my tac vest or anywhere else for that matter, to squeak, rattle or shine out in the dark. The darkness, deep shadow and foliage was my protection, where no-one would see me before I saw them, or I would hear them before they became aware of me.

The hidden garden door was the other side of the swimming pool that was about ten by ten metres square and obviously, for the sole use of the president's family and close friends on hot summer days. In the darkness, you would hear water constantly sprayed over the pool to keep it fresh and clean for presumably, there were no chemicals available.

On night patrol, I would have to brush aside the ivy and locate the door handle, turn it and step through into another world of singing crickets, sparkling fireflies and other sounds that at first, I did not recognise. At first, that would alarm, then delight my senses as I waited and tuned into my Stygian surroundings.

First, my hearing, as I listened to the zephyrs of air gently stirring the leaves and in turn, irritating the branches as I learned to recognise and understand the variations of the sounds. The leaves themselves as they brushed over my skin and clothing and the differences in their touch and the clingy, silky sensation of spiders' webs and the illusive, glancing touch of a moth's wing as it, or was it something else, flittered across my face?

Then, as my sight adjusted, I welcomed the darkness that took on shapes and movement and when my other senses understood these, I relaxed and moved on stronger and confident.

I was on a narrow pathway through this dense foliage which I knew was there as I would use the path when on days at Cactus, although now unseen in the darkness, but with my senses tangibly making their winding way to the first clearing and another huge mango tree.

The clearing would be bathed in moonlight, making it a no-go ground for me to step onto as the mango tree's shadow had not yet reached my pathway. I would step back into the foliage and then sideways and slowly, silently and gently, work my way through and reach the other side of the clearing.

It was at about this time into my patrol, I would hear in my radio earpiece the reassuring double click Ed would make on his speak button, asking if I was alright and I would quickly single click my speak button on the lead from my radio, signalling I was. The feel-good factor I would get from those metallic sounds never failed to put a smile on my face in the darkness. What a sight I must have made, dressed and armed to kill, with camouflage stripes across my grinning face and another reason why in the dark, I did not want the guard in his sanger to hear my approach before I whistled my presence, the sight of me stepping from the night would have sent him into convulsions.

Circling the clearing and just a few further metres on, were the flight of concrete steps climbing up to the sanger. The path approaching the steps would be strewn with leaves, rubbish from the guards and other debris, waiting to announce my presence by amplifying my footfall. So, I would turn my boots on their outer edges and slowly walk on the outer rims of the soles cutting out almost all sound my footsteps would have made.

There I would stop and listen for any sound coming from upstairs in the sanger. Sometimes there would be no sound, sometimes I would hear gentle snoring, I have even heard a radio playing, would you believe. No sound at all, I liked; it either meant the guard was awake and alert, or asleep and not alert, or more importantly he was either not there at all or dead.

I did not like dead!

That would have meant someone had killed him and so where were the killer or killers now?

Waiting for me in the darkness?

I softly whistled and immediately heard the guard stir and whispered, "Packy problem," and hearing the guard repeat my call, mounted the steps, my rifle up to my shoulder, hot, should there be any nasty surprise waiting for me.

The guard was sat with his back to me as I entered the sanger and briefly turned to me and acknowledged my presence. I recognised him as the guard who's cut hand, I hand cleaned and dressed a few days previously in this same sanger.

He lifted the hand and showed me the wound. The dressing had long gone of course, it would have quickly got too dirty to continue its purpose anyway and I examined the wound site by the light of my torch. He had, at least, kept the wound clean, it was healing and with no sign of infection, something that I was really concerned about.

I gave him the thumbs up signal and from my small first aid kit smeared some antibacterial cream on and stuck a large sticking plaster over the site.

He said quietly, "Merci monsieur," and I patted his shoulder.

As I stepped over to look out from the sanger over the tropical countryside beyond, the moon suddenly emerged from a cloud and swathed us and the sanger in bright moonlight.

We both shrank back seeking shadow and cover.

I would stay a few minutes and dig into my shirt breast pocket and give the guard a piece of chewing gum. The guard would nod his thanks, quickly unwrap the gum and put it into his mouth, then sit back in his chair happily chewing.

On reaching the bottom of the steps I would repeat my funny walk with feet on their outer edges and follow the path back to the clearing and the huge mango tree.

There I would crouch in shadow and listen and watch for a few minutes satisfying myself the rhythm of the clearing and surrounding trees, and foliage had not been altered by the presence of others.

Then, moving slowly to my right and keeping to the shadows, I would pass behind the mango and follow the wider pathway to the other sanger and another guard to reassure and comfort with my presence and pass on some chewing gum.

The last stop on my patrol was the main gate itself. I would walk openly down the drive from the inner gate towards the main gate hoping the guards at the gate would have seen me approaching, again not wanting to frighten them with my sudden appearance. Usually about five or six, some who would be dozing in their greatcoats, inside the guard posts, one on either side of the gates or huddled round a brazier of coals seeking warmth from the night chill.

So, there I was, shirt sleeved, long sleeves for protection from the mosquitoes, a lanolin gel on my hands, face and neck, again for the mosquitoes and perspiring after my patrol in the warm tropical night.

We never, in my time, had an attack on Cactus, which I still find surprising, as it was clearly a soft target when compared with the National Palace. But as I understood it at the time, to the president's enemies, whoever held the National Palace, owned the country.

Chapter 10

Security Advance Party

We had already been waiting a couple of hours in the heat of the afternoon for our counterparts, the Haitian Secret Service. They were invariably late, taking too much time to get themselves together and get going. So often, either at the palace or at Cactus, we would have our vehicle lined up behind the two presidential vehicles. There were always two identical presidential vehicles in the motorcade, hopefully to confuse any shooters. Our chase car driver would be sat behind the wheel and others of our close protection team for that day would be deployed round the president's vehicle, ready to give body cover when he appeared from inside his residence.

Our American colleagues would call this, 'maximum standby'. Usually it was the first lady who would ask impatiently, "Are they here yet?" and I would find myself answering, "On their way, Ma'am." She would give me a knowing cynical smile and roll her eyes. Whoever it was inside the president's residence detailed to give our Haitian comrades the tip that the president was moving was frequently late in doing so and that would result in an untidy scramble to get to their vehicle and positions. They never did quite grasp the ten-minute rule.

Recently, a young and new member to the Haitian Secret Service had shot himself accidentally. The story goes that this recruit was demonstrating to his girlfriend how he could twirl his pistol round his trigger finger before slotting it into its holster. Unfortunately, the weapon he was issued was a

Glock. The Glock's safety catch is built into the trigger, so if the trigger is pulled deliberately, the weapon will fire. This young inexperienced lad would have had no real training on this weapon and clearly did not realise the danger as he twirled the Glock round his trigger finger. Of course, the weapon discharged, the round entering his head under his chin and into and existing his brain. He was dead before he and the Glock hit the ground. How dreadfully sad.

We needed to leave the National Palace and start the long and perilous journey to Les Cayes on the south coast of the southern claw of Haiti before dark.

It was an early Friday evening, a few days before Christmas and now beginning to get dark. No one, not us or our Haitian counterparts wanted to make this journey in the dark. The journey in daylight was going to be dangerous enough without being told *"They are waiting for you. They know you are coming."* But at night, in the darkness, we were asking for trouble, and not for the first time, I had the impression our Haitian companions would not have even considered the journey if we Blancs had not been with them. We were heading deep into *Indian Country,* and we had not been invited!

Apart from the vigilantes, otherwise known as OPs or Organisation Popular that make themselves responsible for the security and summary justice in their communities, their towns and villages through the power of the gun, there is, of course, the mulatto establishment that owned the land, the farms and plantations and the roads we and the president would travel on. There is also the fear all Haitians have travelling the countryside in the darkness. For it is then that they believe that the spirits of the dead abound, and zombies walk the land. A very real and present fear for these people. This was the region we would be travelling through for the next three days, very anti-Aristide and the Voodoo drums would beat, and there would be screams in the night. We were expecting trouble!

So finally, just as the darkness came, our three Haitian counterparts appeared, got into their vehicle, started up, turned on the red emergency lights and siren, and waved at us to follow them.   We took our time getting into our vehicle. They wanted us with them, so they would not be too far ahead before they stopped and waited for us. Our Greek driver and former US marine combat medic Chris was waiting for us. Lee, a former Delta Force tunnel rat and assassin from the Vietnam war was our detail leader, then Brett and I made up the advance party. Chris and Ed were with the main party, escorting the president and first lady with their entourage and would leave the following morning.

The security advance party is a unit that travels ahead of the president's party securing, or 'making safe', each of their destinations, then radioing our colleagues in the close protection unit that all is safe for them to enter the locations they are heading for. As soon as they would arrive at one destination, we would stay long enough to make sure all was okay, then leapfrog on to the next village or town the president was due to visit and secure and if need be, *"Cleanse."*

The three towns on this mission were firstly Les Cayes, which we would secure that night on our arrival and where we would await the president's motorcade, then on to Port Salut and finally, Tiburon on the tip of the south claw of the island, plus all the dozen or so villages along the coast between the towns. It was a very remote area and if we were to run into trouble down here, we were all on our own. So, this task was to be done by the book, no short cuts and no prisoners. I was happy to have Lee as this detail's team leader. He knew the island and the people and spoke creole.

The drive from the National Palace through Port au Prince was at a feverish pace, as Chris tried to keep up with our Haitian counterparts. It seemed they were desperate to get through the grim and murderous suburb of Carrefour without stopping for traffic lights, other traffic or people walking beside the road. I had the feeling that if stopped and their vehicle was recognised by its palace number plates, or if they themselves were recognised, they would be dragged from their vehicle and given the fiery necklace. They were nervous, and I really could not blame them for their reckless driving style. Was this why we had waited so long for them at the National

Palace, had they wanted to drive through Port au Prince in the dark?

Umm.

Two days previously, Lee and I, with two Haitian police officers, had boarded our Huey helicopter and flew to Les Cayes, firstly, to drop off a fifty-gallon barrel of aviation fuel which was strapped to seating next to me as we were to have 'top cover' during the president's progression through the countryside, and second, so the police could have a wander through the town and sniff the air, to see what the reception would be like when the president arrived. As I dangled my legs out of the helicopter's open side, my thoughts were not so much on any bad guys below who would take pot shots at us but if one of the incoming rounds hit the barrel. For then, we would all go to heaven in a great ball of fire, and I found myself humming Jerry Lee Lewis's hit, *Great Balls of Fire*. Lee, forever the pessimist looked at the barrel then at me and said, "If the fucking Jesus nut don't get us, that fucking barrel of fuel will! You ever seen one of those explode?" It was not unusual for the Huey to take fire, and more than once when I had been in the air, I would hear the odd round strike.

"Thanks Lee, I really needed to hear that," I laughed, "Anyway, what's the fucking Jesus nut?"

Lee gave me a knowing smile, kept me waiting several seconds for dramatic effect, then replied with a heavy lugubrious drawl, "The Jesus nut, my friend, is what holds this machine together, it connects the rotor blades to the engine." He changed tone and became more animated, "If that nut fails, the blades separate, and you go to heaven," Lee pointed at me, paused and looked me sadly in the eyes, "and I go to hell!" Lee, the former tunnel rat and later assassin, presumably at the behest of another agency, would show us letters from LBJ thanking him for 'services'. Then he'd tell us how he would enter the house of the target, kill them, the wife and children, and whoever else was in the house, including any cats or dogs, even the parrot, if they had one. The murders were designed to strike terror in those who were enemies of the US. Lee could not sleep, and now lived in his own private hell.

Lee was an excellent shot, once chasing two house breakers from his home in Petionville, firing two shots from his pistol and killing both.

Packy problem!

We landed on a football pitch somewhere at the edge of town, unloaded the barrel, hiding it in a shed, and the police walked off towards the town. We stayed with the helicopter guarding it and the French pilot. I asked him what he thought of the barrel on his aircraft, he gave a gallic shrug, rolled his eyes to heaven and said sarcastically, "Packy problem." Our French helicopter pilots were all former French special forces flyers and knew their stuff. The police officers hastily returned only a few minutes later saying everything was okay.

"Packy problem!"

"Yeah right!" I thought.

But then, like us, they were seriously at risk, and visions of the fiery necklace would have been in the forefront of their minds. They were big city boys from Port au Prince, so the countryside was alien, and probably very frightening, particularly as just outside every town and village out here, there would be a small collection of straw huts with two flags flapping in the breeze above the huts, one white, for white magic and the other black, for black magic. After all, us Blancs only had to worry about dying in a gunfight hopefully, they had Baron Samadi, who would take their souls and turn them into zombies. I was forever finding it too easy to turn my nose up at these people until I came to understand that Haitians, particularly the poor and uneducated and the country folk, live in their own spiritual world, with the Roman Catholic Church and Voodoo all mixed up together, very heady stuff. Every aspect of their lives controlled by the spirits, the breeze that dries their washing, the flowers that grow in their gardens, to the demons who rattle their windowpanes on a dark stormy night.

They were nervous and obviously did not want to go too far from Lee and I, or the helicopter. Some locals had wandered over and stood some yards off, staring at us two Blancs and the pilot. The police spoke to these people who continued to gaze at us in awe and wonderment. I think the police had probably told them that we were zombies. We were white, the colour of death in Voodoo.

Anyway, back to the mission.

We had made it through Carrefour along the Hoover highway and out of Port au Prince without incident, even driven through Petit Goave with not a whisper of trouble. In the back, I started to relax, looking over at Brett next to me, he was asleep. Typical, the British squaddie with nothing to do. Eat, sleep or use the loo! If there was one to use.

I was now feeling tired and my eyes were starting to roll round my head. Making myself more comfortable, I must have dropped off. *"Wake me up when we get there,"* I mused.

"Guns up! Watch yourselves!" Lee called from the front of our vehicle.

I came out of my doze wide awake, grabbed my M16 resting barrel down beside my left leg, and brought the stock up to my left shoulder and flicked off the safety catch. The rifle did not need racking, we always carried our weapons 'hot'. Through the window screen, I saw the Haitian Secret Service vehicle come to a stop, and we pulled up a few feet behind. Brett had come to the ready with me, like the old soldier he was.

What I saw next sent a shiver down my spine, for there, to our front and straddling the road, were at least three dozen armed men, dimly illuminated by moonlight in the misty night, giving them an eerie, spooky appearance.

All four of us immediately rolled out from our vehicle, weapons up and showing we were ready for anything they had to offer. There really is no point in being shy and retiring at times like this. Timidity just encourages the threat. Better to die roaring like a lion, than bleating like a lamb. Or so I was telling myself! Besides, a vehicle is an easy point of aim for any attacking force, just shoot at the vehicle and you are bound to hit someone inside.

Our Haitian companions were out of their vehicle, pistols in hands, fear on their faces.

Lee said quietly, "Cover me. I'll find out what's going on," and walked forward to join the Haitian Secret Service.

Lee spoke good creole; he was married to a Haitian he had met in the US. I had asked him why he had settled in Haiti what with all the opportunities and contacts he had back home from his previous life in Delta Force. He shrugged and answered, "I thought she said she was from Tahiti!"

I chose to leave my rifle in our vehicle hoping not to spook these men and moved forward to cover Lee's back and for the first time, realised the men were not black Haitians but mulattos, Aristides's sworn enemies. Lee turned, saw me and whispered, "OPs." As one approached me and said, "No problem man. We're just dealing with guys who have been holding up cars." He spoke perfect American English, and pointed to three young men lying face down, arms outstretched and whimpering on the side of the road.

Another man began to beat them with a plank of wood, and the three of them began to scream, screams full of pain and fear, and I saw there were blood stained nails in the plank.

I turned back to the mulatto and raised my eyebrows questionably. He shrugged and said, "What the fuck man, we're going to kill them anyway."

Lee pulled me away saying quietly, "Nothing we can do here, let's go while we can."

Our Haitian counterparts were already moving back to their vehicle.

I followed Lee when suddenly a gunshot split the heavy night air, and the fingers of my left hand reached for and touched the pistol holstered on my duty belt as I turned to see one of the other OPs leaning over the three youths on the ground. He had a pistol in his hand, and then fired the weapon twice more shooting into the back of the heads of the other two.

I felt an urgent tug on my arm. It was Lee and we hurried back to our vehicle. I was angry, having had just witnessed the murder of three young men. *Yeah, we were deep in Indian Country alright!*

We all got back into our vehicle and followed our companions who were, by this time, speeding away from this grisly scene.

Brett asked, "What happened?"

Lee shook his head, "We were lucky there."

I answered Brett, "Nothing like a summary execution before bedtime."

Very clearly outgunned, we could expect no support from the Haitian Secret Service, they had taken to their heels, and to be very honest with you dear reader, I did not feel much like dying that evening. For that is what would have happened if I had protested and tried to intervene, I would not only have got myself, but my other comrades killed. The whole incident had left me angry at the casual slaughter of three youths, and how fast lives could be snatched away in the blink of an eye. But also, I felt disgust at the arrogant way these vigilantes had dealt with the incident. Okay, beatings and killings are a part of their world, and the taking of life spontaneous and nonchalant. It was all around us, all the time, and so to me, it appeared that sudden death does not have the same impact on the population as it does in the US, or northern Europe.

There was no more dozing in the back of the vehicle for the remainder of the journey to our first destination.

In more affluent times, Les Cayes was a party town with private beaches, bungalows and bars for the visiting wealthy from Port au Prince and France. Not now! The private beaches were deserted, the bungalows empty, and the bars just have cats and caretakers lounging in them. On National Holidays, the wealthy mulattos would briefly bring them to life again and after, Les Cayes would return to its long desolate sleep just like the Ibo Lele Hotel.

Our small party arrived in the town sometime after midnight, and there was not a soul to be seen. The Tivoli beach lights were on, giving us a forlorn, pale, sickly welcome, and telling us at least that we were expected. But the dim glow of the lights gave the town even more of an impression it had been asleep for years.

As we turned into the square, we saw it was festooned with bunting and banners welcoming "Tidi!" Little Father from the grass roots black Haitians. The church there was where the president would meet the town's dignitaries and clergy before taking mass. This was where we would wait for the main party to arrive, sometime in the morning before driving on to the next location.

The night was still, the square empty and what we could see of the town was empty. We were alone, but again, I had the uncomfortable and powerful sensation we were being watched, dozens of pairs of eyes examining us from the shadowy darkness. Time enough at dawn to show the residents that it was the Blancs who were here in their town, and we entered the church, unrolled our sleeping bags and settled down for a few hours' sleep. In the morning, we would source coffee and bread, and hopefully a third world egg or two to fill our stomachs and then secure the square.

Our Haitian comrades had told us there would be no problem in Les Cayes as it was the birthplace of the president's mother, there would be problems in

Port Salut though, where President Aristide himself was born.

So, settling into my sleeping bag, I drifted off, cuddling my M16, with images of three youths being executed in my head.

It was early, the priests had arrived and were preparing for the morning service. They smiled at us and briefly, I thought we might be offered coffee and bread. No, following their greeting we were ignored, and so we dressed quickly, rounded up our gear and went to our vehicle.

We were to meet our Haitian team at the church shortly before the president was due to arrive, round about midday, assuming they were not late. From the church, He was expected to visit the birthplace of his mother. She was still alive and living with his brother and wife on the outskirts of Port au Prince, not far from the president's own private residence, code name Cactus.

Chris, our driver, locked the vehicle and the four of us scouted the area round the church, so we could understand the layout of the town and identify the road the president's motorcade would approach from. We were fully armed, myself with the M16 and my three companions carrying their Uzi Subs. It was important that the locals should see us and understand that we meant business. We would wave and smile at them, but they had to know it was a smile on the faces of tigers! Any anti-Aristide elements in the town would hopefully, think twice about any disruption or attack. We were expecting Port Salut would be the hard nut to deal with, but that was to be later that afternoon, let us deal with any problems in one town at a time.

Arriving at the park where three days earlier Lee and I had stored the extra fuel for our 'top cover', an elderly lady approached and invited us to her small *gingerbread* house on the edge of the park. She stepped through her doorway and beckoned us in. We, in turn, placed our right hands over our hearts and on the threshold of her doorway, said respectfully, "Honour," and stepped inside. Then, she invited us to sit on her wooden chairs. She gave us each a cup of coffee, dark black coffee from locally grown coffee beans and bread made by herself. All these years later, I can still remember the taste of her coffee. The only time I have ever able to get anywhere near repeating the taste was to spend some £40 or so on a small packet of Jamaican Blue Mountain Coffee.

Walking back to the church, we noticed small groups of locals gathering in the streets obviously wanting to see the Blancs who had arrived in their town. The only light skinned people they would have ever come across were the wealthy mulattos who would spend weekends here. The children had been given a day off from school, and they were more forward in approaching us and smiling. In this part of the world, it would usually indicate everything was normal.

But "They" were always watching.

We received a radio call advising us the motorcade was ten minutes out from Les Cayes, and Brett and I deployed to the square's approaches, while Lee stood on the church steps so our team could see him and know all was good. Our Haitian counterparts were nowhere to be seen.

The motorcade swept pass me and stopped at the church, Ed and Chris giving me a nod and wave as they passed, it was good to see them both again.

The president stepped from his vehicle and the crowd surged forward, a sea of smiling faces. He and the first lady greeted them, allowing those nearby to touch the president's hand, and I was reminded of other walkabouts especially in Port au Prince, where young tearful mothers would bring their recently dead children for their "Little Father" to touch.

Inside the church, the president and first lady took mass. The church was full of course, but cooler than the outside. Tropical churches have open sides with huge ceiling fans allowing a cool flow of air. Lee indicated to Chris, our driver, to bring our vehicle into the square, he now wanted us to leapfrog onto Port Salut and find out what was waiting for us there. Gale told us to watch ourselves, telling us that that president had insisted in taking mass there as well. Taking mass in a town's church or cathedral was His way of saying *These people do not dictate to me!*

We stopped at a small shop on the outskirts of Les Cayes and bought bread and hard-boiled eggs for our lunch, paying in US dollars, probably ten times more than her goods were worth. The dear lady could not stop thanking us, "Oh merci, oh merci." I smiled at her and thought *"Make friends, not enemies,"* and we drove on towards Port Salut. My American colleagues, hardcore former US marines and special forces, had their own saying, all be it remotely similar, *"Be courteous and friendly, but have a plan to kill everyone you meet."*

Umm!

But to be fair though, that phrase spoken by a US marine commandant is so often taken out of context from its original meaning.

He was to meet his people inside the town's vegetable market, show himself and then take mass a short walk away in the church. We drove fast and hard into town, our sirens screaming and red lights flashing, wanting to give the impression we meant business. No prisoners here! On reaching the marketplace, we stopped by a stage erected for the president's visit. A nephew of Mildred, the first lady, was rigging the sound equipment and greeted us saying, "Glad you're here." He looked over at the gathering crowd adding, "He don't have a lot of friends here." I forget his name now, but we would see him regularly round the palace and private residence, fixing anything to do with cameras or sound equipment. He was Haitian American and spoke perfect American English, but also Haitian creole and French, so easily passing as a mulatto and therefore, could move freely with reasonably safety through the countryside.

The market was busy, market stalls piled full of vegetables, most I recognised but some I did not, and the market women were friendly, singing out their greetings and shouting *"Tidi."* I called out the greeting *"Bonjour,"* to a pair of ladies behind their market stall not realising it was now the afternoon. They, of course, were bemused but replied politely *"Bonjour,"* as I realised the time and gushingly called, *''Bonsoir! Je suis desole.''* These wonderful ladies broke down in gales of laughter, waved their arms and shouted to me, *"Bonsoir!''* And I was again reminded of other times and other places where I had met local people that were just like me and everyone I knew back home. They got on with their lives and cherished their families.

But others in that square were not so happy to see us and stood watching us with blank expressions. Watching us and talking to others, as the market began to fill with locals, their faces smiling, and clearly anxious to see their "Tidi."

Lee looked over the varying crowd and turned to me saying, "He should be okay in here, especially with SWAT in his retinue. But the longer he takes to get here, the longer "They" have to get themselves organised." He shrugged adding, "Okay, 'guns up', watch yourselves! Marty, post yourself at the entrance, but stay in our line of sight. We're here guarding the stage. No prisoners Marty. Mean business!"

Standing about fifty yards or so from my companions at the entrance of the market place was uncomfortable, I felt exposed, although the three of us had line of site of each other and so once again, I found myself reciting my old chant when alone, exposed and feeling in danger, "Chin up, plenty of swagger!" as Chris appeared armed with his Uzi and stood post with me, asking, "Marty, you see our counterparts?"

"No Chris, they have bottled it!"

"Bottled it, Marty!"

"Yeah, bottled it! I'll explain later. You cover over there, and I'll cover the rest mate. And Chris," he turned and looked up at me, "Thanks for coming, I was lonely here by myself."

The presidential motorcade roared into town, sirens screaming and lights flashing, the two motorcycle outriders and leading UV with its 50 Cal (calibre) machine gun mounted on the back, always got people's attention. I doubted the bloody great thing would fire, or if it did, it would probably jam after a few rounds, and more importantly, would the operator, who was, as usual, clinging to the gun for dear life, or the driver, be able to clear the stoppage?

Still, it looked impressive.

The outrider spotted Chris, our driver and me at the market entrance and the motorcade drove through the entrance portico and into the marketplace. I spotted Chris and Ed in our chase vehicle, briefly made eye contact as they passed my position, then turned back to the street we were both covering.

I listened to the opening and closing of vehicles doors as our team, with their Haitian counterparts, would be screening and escorting the president and his first lady onto the stage and I closed my ears to the clutter of noise coming from the market. There were more than enough armed people surrounding the president to deal with anything inside the marketplace and concentrated on the street.

Brett joined us saying, "He's secure. Anything going on out here?"

I crossed my fingers, "Not yet mate." And continued watching a small crowd that was gathering on the opposite side of the road, some one hundred and fifty yards away. There was something about their body language that held my attention.

Then this crowd suddenly began to disperse into buildings and alleys behind them and I called, "Possible X-rays at two o'clock, stand by!"

Both Brett and Chris immediately dropped prone on the footpath as I took cover by one of the portico's pillars. The street began to empty rapidly. There followed a volley of small arms fire from the location of the crowd who had held my attention, nothing accurate but rounds were smacking into the wall close to the portico. The three of us returned fire pouring several rounds from each of us into their positions, showing we meant business and that we were not going anywhere. The opposition kept up their steady rate of fire, and we slowed our rate, only firing single rounds at identified targets.

Lee appeared laughing, and shouted, "I leave you guys alone for a few minutes and you upset the locals." He crouched beside me and said, "Our guys are evacuating the president, Gale asked we hold for five minutes as rear guard, then follow." He turned his head and nodded to the motorcade now loading the president and first lady hastily, and turned and looked at me shrewdly with his knowing eyes and asked, "You up for this?"

I looked at my other two companions and thought my answer to Lee would involve them as well, arguably unfair to them but needs must. "Brett watch yourself, motorcade coming through. Chris get our vehicle and follow the motorcade out and wait for us here." Then eyed Lee saying, "Okay, they got five."

Lee gently thumped me on the shoulder smiling and said, "Let's do it!"

I called to Brett, "Let's conserve our ammo Brett, we're here for another five mikes"

"Yeah Mart, at least my tac vest will be lighter," he replied and continued his controlled rate of fire.

The road was now deserted as the motorcade again swept through the portico at speed with some fire from the occupants of vehicles in the motorcade, all shooting at the wrong buildings of course, breaking some windows and scaring the crap out of the innocent folk taking cover. What else? At least none of the firing came from our chase vehicle I noted proudly and caught sight of Ed and Chris. They were looking the other way and did not see me. For some reason I still cannot explain, my two friends and me unable to make eye contact at that instant in time left me saddened, and in my mind, I wondered if I would ever see them again.

Thank the Lord, the 50 Cal did not open-up, its gunner too busy hanging on for dear life, besides, it would have knocked down any building its huge rounds may have hit.

The shooters rate of fire dramatically increased, and Brett shouted over the crackle of gunfire, "That pissed them off!"

"Okay," Lee shouted, "Let's remind them we're still here!" and the three of us commenced a steady rate of fire for a few seconds, then slowed to single shots again.

Once again, the opposition did not want to expose themselves and take ground and we took comfort in knowing that this time "They" again were not organised or lead by a professional. *"Thanks for that!"* I thought, but it was the longest five minutes I had ever spent in my current lifetime!

Eventually Lee called, "Mount up!" and the three of us sprang up and speedily climbed into our waiting vehicle, and Chris roared away, following the motorcade, taking the opposition completely by surprise.

"Where's our 'top cover', Lee?" I asked. We could have done with our Huey and a couple of our counter snipers giving any shooters second thoughts.

Lee shrugged.

We were deep in *Indian Country*!

Lee took a call from Gale telling us we would RV at Port au Piment, the president would have lunch with the town's officials, and stay the night at the rectory.

"Sounds like we sleep under the stars," grumbled Brett, "Still, at least it's not with the fishes!" he added, brightening up.

I was handing out bottled water from our stash in the back and realised I was hungry again and rummaged in my day sack and found my supply of nutty chocolate. "We need to source some real food, not just bread and eggs."

"Where there's eggs, there's chickens, Marty." It was Chris, "And where there's bread, there's bread ovens!"

"Yes!" we shouted in unison.

"Leave it to me," smiled Chris.

Port au Piment was a small town, and as we arrived, the motorcade was sighted from the church that appeared almost too big for the town. Big church, small town, but it would be full every Sunday for mass, and we had passed the usual collection of straw huts on the edge of town, two flag poles, one white flag, one black flag. Voodoo and the Roman Catholic Church side by side.

Ed and Chris were at the church doors, so presumably the president was meeting the priests inside, Gale and Mark would be with him.

Our vehicle was parked tactically, facing back along the road we had just travelled. We dismounted, and I waved at my two friends, then found cover and waited for any sign of the shooters from Port Salut. It was hot, although I was in the shade of a huge mango tree and lying prone, I soon felt myself starting to get sleepy. I stood and shook myself awake and walked round the tree looking for somewhere I could sit up, but still in cover, and finding a perfect spot, I sat with my back at one of the large roots with another large root covering my position.

A small child, a girl, appeared carrying a banana leaf with a sliced mango on it and offered the leaf to me. This beautiful little girl was wearing a dress of printed flowers, her hair was plaited, her little shoes polished brightly. She gave me a shy smile, as I took the sliced mango from her, then quickly fumbled in my shirt pocket, found a dollar bill and gave it to her. Her smile got wider, and I turned and saw other children handing out banana leaves with sliced mangos to my friends. The mango was delicious.

Lee came over and squatted beside me, "He's flying back to Port au Prince from Tiburon tomorrow with Gale, we'll drive back in convoy with the rest. Gale says our counterparts and police are crapping themselves about driving in the dark especially back through Petit Goave."

That night under the mango tree was a long one, especially as our counterparts again warned us, *"They are coming, be ready!"* That piece of intel was beginning to wear a bit thin, but they did get Port Salut right, although it did not amount to much. I was thinking we could have probably held them off just by pulling faces at them.

During the evening, Chris brought us a roast chicken each, that's third world roast chicken, our sparrows are bigger. It was delicious and did not touch the sides as it went down, and each of us managed to get a couple of hours sleep while the others watched and waited.

Watching and waiting in the dark is a whole different experience especially in the tropics when in the small hours the temperature drops, and the ground begins to give up the heat it's absorbed during the day, a mist begins to rise, and the moon casts its eerie light glowing spookily through the mist. The lush vegetation so enjoyed in the daylight plays tricks with your eyes in the darkness, and the watcher starts to see shapes and movement that may or may not be human. And so, you begin to understand the Haitian dread of the night with the Voodoo thing going on in their heads. There were times during my watch that night, as the Voodoo drums began, I almost convinced myself "They" were here, but a quick rub of my eyes and another look and everything came back into focus. Perhaps it was only the breeze playing with the mist or perhaps the spirits playing with my mind, or just *smoke and mirrors!* Strange thing about the drums is I was never aware of them starting and could not remember them stopping, and so consequently, in my mind, they were just there in the background all the time, in the darkness.

Weird!

Sunup, and there was Ed and Chris bringing us coffee and bread they had sourced from the priests. It was going to be another long day, I thought, as I wolfed down the bread. "You get any kip?" Ed asked, eyeing the road from Port Salut. "Couple of hours. What's on today?" I asked and saw Gale chatting to Lee.

Ed looked at me seriously, his expression showing concern, "Well Caesar and Cleopatra are flying back from Tiburon as you know, but our Haitians are really scared of the drive back. We're going to have to nurse maid them through the night."

Yes of course, it's going to be a night drive back to Port au Prince.

"It's going to be 'Wacky Races' with that lot, it's going to be more dangerous than running into "Them".

Ed said looking at Chris, "We must get back. Stay safe Martyn, see you back at the Mountain Noir." He held out his hand, I took it and we both gently squeezed.

Chris and I both quickly looked at each other, no words needed to be said, and he gave me a nod and the thumbs up and walked away with Ed.

Lee called the three of us over to his position. He lit a cigarette, took that first all-important drag and blew the smoke over his left shoulder away from us. "Here's the deal. There are three villages between here and Tiburon. We'll be leap frogging through them and meeting up with the others at Tiburon. Gale seems to think there shouldn't be any problems until the drive back, especially going through Petit Goave. Well, let's worry about that when we get there. Yeah?"

We nodded and started to get our kit together as Chris, our medic as well as our driver, walked off to our vehicle.

"How you are doing Brett?" Lee asked.

The real South Londoner, Brett came shining through, "Well!" he said in mock seriousness, "I could murder a cup of tea, Lee."

"For fuck's sake," muttered Lee, walking off shaking his head.

"Not sure he gets our humour, Brett." I said chuckling.

"Don't know what he's missing," grinned Brett.

Within a few minutes, we were loaded into our vehicle and travelling west. We made good time getting into the countryside where we crossed a shallow, fast flowing river, some fifty yards or so wide, and there, on the far side was a beautiful young girl, half naked, washing herself in one of the deeper pools. It was a timeless, beguiling scene in the dappled early morning sunlight. Being the rough lot we were, we shouted out in unison, "Ooh Ahh!" as this vision of Aphrodite, the Greek goddess of pleasure, proudly stood up, gave us a bright innocent smile and waved. In that fleeting moment, this triumphant image of youth and beauty was gone, as we reached the far bank and drove on and we were left wondering was that real or was it all just a mirage.

No, it was real, we all saw it, or was it the jungle spirits playing their tricks again with *smoke and mirrors?*

As planned, we leap frogged through the villages, stopping briefly, while Lee chatted to the locals, satisfying himself it was safe to radio the all clear. Finally, we reached Tiburon in mid-afternoon, knowing the president's motorcade was about an hour behind us.

We drove through the neat small town to the church and waited.

The town had a quiet air of comfort, not exactly wealth but obviously not poverty stricken. Dozens of school children were in the small dusty square, lined up with the younger, smaller children in the front with the older ones to the back. They were chatting and laughing together as all children the world over do. Teachers, all smartly dressed, the men in suits, white shirts and ties, and the ladies in black skirts and white blouses, patrolled the eager giggling lines of children. An older man appeared, I guessed he was the headmaster, and stood before the lines of children. They quickly came to a respectful silence as he held his hands in the air and gently gestured to the children. They began to sing, a magical lilting sound that was punctuated by a soft lingering sigh at the end of each verse. Then, they hummed the song's tune before singing the next verse. It brought a lump to my throat as I listened. There I was, at the very south western edge of Haiti, looking over the shark invested waters of the Western Caribbean, Tiburon is Spanish for shark, and the end of the world for poor Haitians, and here in this peaceful enchanting place, I stood fighting back my tears, listening to singing that must have come from heaven.

Silly old fool!

The greeting sung by the school children was watched by the president and his first lady, who then spoke with town elders and priests in the church. The scene was ethereal, and I had to stop myself blubbering and pull myself together and concentrate on doing my job.

His personal helicopter had landed in the square, its pilot, a former US marine, was waiting by his aircraft. We had been told our Huey had developed rotor problems and was back at base being repaired. I was watching Lee, Gale and Franc Joseph, the president's personal bodyguard, fixer and confidant in a huddle, deep in conversation.

"Hmm, what's being cooked up now?" I thought to myself and could see our Haitian counterparts

nervously glancing at their watches, for it was now late afternoon and the sun was starting to go down.

Lee collected Brett and Chris and they walked over to my position, watching the road from Port Salut. We were all well rested over the last few hours, although we had not had any more sleep, had not managed to source any food and had now to ration our water. But it was the last day and only a seven-hour drive back to Port au Prince and some real food, plenty of water, a shower, and a real bed. It's the small things in life that keep you going.

"I've got some good news, and some bad news guys," Lee said grimacing.

Each of us said nothing, waiting for what we were about to be hit with.

"The good news is......we'll be driving back with Mark, Ed and Chris."

"Here it comes," interrupted Brett.

"They'll take lead vehicle in the convey to control the speeds these crazy bastards will be wanting to travel." I was watching Lee trying hard to choose his next words carefully, "And we are drag." He ended in a rush of words and stood before us wide-eyed, no doubt wondering how we were going to take this plan.

"Drag?" the three of us responded.

"Yeah, drag. Gale and Franc Joseph are worried that the convey will get lost and spread all over the southern claw. Don't sound as if he's too worried about the men, he wants the vehicles back at the palace. So, us front and back, will keep them bunched up. It's guns-up all the way home guys."

This meant of course, any attack on the convey and we would be stuck in the rear with our arses hanging out, and separated by well over a mile from Ed, Chris and Mark, there were sixteen vehicles, separated in anti-ambush mode, assuming our Haitian comrades understood that concept. I looked over at our Haitian counterparts who each had a worried expression of their faces and kept looking up at the sun getting lower and lower in the sky.

"Okay, 'Whisky Uniform', but let's give them fifteen minutes. Mount up!" called Lee, as we watched the helicopter climb in the air, taking the president and his first lady back to Port au Prince.

'Whisky uniform' was radio speak for 'wheels up', meaning the aircraft had taken off, and fifteen minutes was time allowed in case of any problem with the aircraft meaning it had to return to the airfield.

Ed's team were moving to the front of the convey when the Haitian Secret Service vehicles roared away ignoring their last orders. Lee muttered, "Fuck them," waiting with the rest of the convoy and counted down the fifteen-minute time protocol, then began our drive back to Port au Prince.

We were on country roads, rough, bumpy and dusty, about an hour into the seven-hour drive. The light was fading, and Chris needed to keep his distance from the vehicle in front, it was supposed to be at least two hundred yards in front of us unless the topography of the road meant the vehicle to our front was out of sight, then that would dictate the distance between vehicles. But our Haitian colleagues in front had no intention of losing sight of us preferring to stick as close as they could. I could not blame them as the thought of the fiery necklace was always in the forefront of our minds out here in the countryside, and they would have heard about the execution of three youths by the opposition.

Suddenly this vehicle swerved to the right and rapidly gained speed as we saw a crowd of some sixty people gathered ahead on our left. Standing out front from this crowd was a tall man probably in his forties, holding what I recognised as a young girl who was lying limp in his arms, her long hair hanging down his right leg, her arms limp and outstretched, her legs dangling. We all came to the full alert as we saw the child had, what appeared to be, a massive head wound. The expression on the face of the man holding her was one of extreme anguish and desperation and seeing us, it was obvious to him we were his last hope of getting the child (was it his daughter?) medical attention.

"Lee, we have to stop and help," I said, knowing what his answer, as our detail leader, would have to be.

"We can't stop Marty. In the blink of an eye, that crowd will turn into a thousand. They'll know we're government people and we'll find ourselves having to shoot our way out, if we get out at all. Drive on Chris, it was probably one of those crazy bastards up front!"

"I'm a trained trauma medic, Lee," pleaded Chris.

"Listen to me guys, if the kid is still alive, it's still six hours to Port au Prince. If she lasts the journey, there's no hospital in Haiti that can manage that injury. She stays with her people." I saw that Lee was as much affected by this as we all were, but this situation needed a leader, and Lee led, "Drive on Chris!"

And so, we left these people who continued to plead with us to stop, and the face of this man who was holding the child still visits me in the night, sometimes waking me from sleep and sometimes just walking through my thoughts when unable to sleep. The incident had left us all deeply affected and depressed, and ever since, I have felt a sense of shame.

But you know, Lee made a good call, he was right to resist our natural instincts. He was right, we almost certainly would have had to fight our way out and killing many of these people in doing so, and if we had made it back to a hospital in Port au Prince with the child alive, there was no one, no doctor, who could have treated her, and no drugs to support her life either.

I understood all this, but today all these years later, that sense of shame and the anguished face of the man cradling this child in his arms has never left me. Perhaps that is my punishment from the Voodoo spirits of Haiti.

And we were still in Indian country.

We were just a few miles outside Petit Goave, the town our Haitian colleagues were terrified of driving through. It had been dark for several hours when the vehicle in our front started pumping its brake lights and pulled to the side of the road. By the light of our headlights was one of the police trucks stopped in the middle of the road with a group of police officers looking at the flat tyre on its rear offside.

We stopped and rolled from our vehicle, 'guns up', as we were surrounded by lush tropical forest. It was not a place any of us would have chosen to change a tyre.

The policewoman appeared to be the senior officer present and spoke to us in American English, "Thank God you're here guys. Can you give us cover while we get this changed?"

Lee stepped forward and said, "Sure, you go ahead."

Brett whispered to me as we separated, "Cor, she's a bit of alright." I was at the front of the police vehicle and crouching down, weapon up, and Brett covered our rear, as the vehicle that had been with us since Tiburon drove round the police truck and sped off.

A cry went up from the police officers and the woman ran up to us and begged us not to leave them.

They were all very frightened. We gritted our teeth and waited.

I listened to Lee reassure them, as I stood in the darkness, off the beams of the headlights and waited for my eyes to adjust. It was a long wait, as they struggled with the tyre, and after a while, my vision started playing tricks with me again, as I began to imagine shapes forming in the jungle around me. I glanced at my watch, I had been out front some twenty minutes or so and knew that every minute that passed gave "Them" time to get at us. Here we were, deep in Indian country with headlights blazing away, giving "Them" our location.

Lee called quietly, "Mount up, Marty."

Music to my ears!

It had begun to rain, a steady drizzle that rapidly soaked everything, and adding another dimension to the darkness of the night. *This could be to our advantage,* I thought and said, "This must really be freaking that lot out."

"Yeah, and the bad guys hopefully don't want to get wet," Lee answered, as we drove through Petit Goave without a peep from the opposition. Again, I found myself thinking, *"Is this the spirits sending the rain, and covering our retreat back to Port au Prince?"* Not the sort of thing I could have said out loud, of course.

We arrived back in Port au Prince in the small hours, had the stand down call from Gale and headed back to our team houses after dropping off Lee at his house, not half a mile from the Ibo Lele.

In my room, I cleared my rifle and stacked it away in the cupboard, I would strip and clean it in the morning. Yes, I know, I know, I really should have done it there and then, but I was truly whacked and needed to lie down in a dark room for a while. I stripped off my clothing and put it outside my door to be washed and ironed and quickly closed the door before that bloody spider came up from its lair and stared at me with its hunter's eyes, big dark round things, forward facing and expressionless. I was too tired to handle the sight of that frightful creature; it gave me the shivers! I carried my duty belt, holster and side arm into the bathroom, hung it on a clothes hook and stepped up to the can. I swear my urine was glowing in the dim bathroom light, it was viscous in colour, I was badly dehydrated. I went back into my bedroom and drank half a litre of bottled water from my bedside cabinet before returning to the bathroom, and stood in the shower for ages allowing the hot running water to cleanse and refresh me, washing off three days of sweat, accumulated dust and dirt, and the residue of fear. I would drink the other half a litre of water after my shower before climbing into bed.

I'm going to shoot that fucking spider!

Chapter 11

Joyous Noel

From a small child, I can always remember that my mother made Christmas a magical time of year and although she was constantly struggling just to make ends meet, the day itself was joyous and that was another gift from mum that has remained with me throughout my life.

How she scraped together enough money for Christmas presents, I still wonder how she did it, but when I awoke on that morning, there were packages wrapped in Christmas paper at the bottom of my bed and a sock stuffed with an orange and a bar of chocolate.

Eagerly opening the packages, first I would look for the Roy Rogers cowboy gun. It had to be a cowboy gun and of course, there it was. I did not need anything else, just that Roy Rogers cowboy gun. Another present, when I was about five or six years old, was a pair of boxing gloves.

I now often speculate that if I had received an encyclopaedia instead, would my life have been different, for I am reminded of written notations from my teachers in schoolwork books, 'Could do better!' usually in red or green ink.

Even as I moved from childhood to a young adult and the beginnings of the life I have lived, Christmas was special and magical, although there were Christmas' when I was not at home with family which were, of course, not quite the same, but I would fortify myself by thinking, I'll do it properly next year when we're all together," though to be honest, there were tears in my eyes.

Haiti was no exception, like the UK, everyone would pass the time of day and finish with 'Happy Christmas!' and so, on my Voodoo island, Christmas was earnestly celebrated by the wealthy, the well off and those who could afford it. In the National Palace, amongst the cleaners, clerks, diplomatic staff and the different security units throughout the week leading up to Christmas, the greeting 'Joyous Noel!' would be heard.

I woke quite early, as is usual for me. It was Christmas morning, I sat up and looked for my presents at the bottom of the bed knowing nothing was there and flopped back down on my back again and let my mind drift off to the other side of the world and my family. My first thoughts were of Gerry and her waking without me beside her again for another year. So many Christmas' had been missed because I was too busy, or off working somewhere horrible. Then thoughts would shift to my two girls and my three wonderful grandsons that I would picture roaring round their homes before dawn looking for presents.

God! I have missed all that and would never get back those missed times. The guilt I felt at those lost Christmas' has never left me. Looking back now, when our children were young and then when the grandchildren we were blessed with came along, I never tucked my girls or grandkids into bed on

Christmas Eve night, nor saw that special excitement and wonder on their faces or had never been there to kiss Gerry at midnight on New Year's Eve.

Now I am sort of semi-retired and available for these wonderful moments, the children, all of them, are, of course, too old, my girls Deb and Mandy and my grandsons who would all roar with laughter should I ask, not seeing the sadness in my face or the tear in my eye.

Yesterday had been my day off and I had taken the opportunity to chill out by the pool at the team house on Mountain Noir and had an early night. For tonight, I was on night duty with Ed, Chris and big Deano, Ed's former comrade in the royal marines.

Deano was forever at his happiest in a rough house and was always ready for anything, whatever the opposition would throw at us. At a summer gathering on the front lawn of the palace, a group from a pro-Aristide street gang became over excited in trying to reach the president and it was Deano who prevented them and so some pushing and pulling commenced. It was Deano who was doing the pushing and pulling, the street gang did not have much of a say in it.

We had taken the president and first lady back inside the palace until things had calmed down and Gale said to us, "Shouldn't we go and get Deano?"

"No!" we replied, "He's enjoying himself."

I looked at my watch, yes it was a bit early, but I knew that the young girl that cleaned our rooms and made our beds would want to get in soon. I have always made my own bed whenever I worked abroad, assuming of course, I had a bed. It was a task I would routinely make myself do, like cleaning my boots and ironing my clothing. But our daily cleaners who also did the washing and ironing for us all, although working long hours every day of the week, still had nothing but a few dollars to feed their families on. So, should that work be denied because some stiff neck like me wanting to do all his own administration, they would have no job and nothing to feed their families on.

I got up, showered, shaved and dressed in a pair of shorts and a Sloppy Joe top, slung my duty belt with its holstered pistol and its spare magazines over my shoulder, put on my flip flops and went to the door, opened it cautiously, first looking and seeing the everything was normal outside and then looked for and saw the spider. Again, we both stared at each other for some seconds, then the demonic creature backed away and disappeared down its hole.

I shuddered and walked on to the kitchen and some breakfast.

Ed and Brett were sat at the kitchen table telling each other war stories and laughing at the other's lies.

"Martyn," greeted Ed who sat in his Y Fronts but still with his duty belt and pistol round his waist, "There's tea in the pot mate."

"Chris is in the pool already! He'll be doing press ups next if you don't stop him," laughed Brett.

"Merry Christmas guys," I said, smiling at my two friends trying to put a brave face on. "I'll get some tea and go and stop Chris before he hurts himself."

We all did phys or physical training when we got up but not before having a prolonged moan and grumble about it and everything else first when we could not get to the gym down at the El Rancho.

I sat in my favourite chair by the side of the pool under the hardwood tree with the orchid growing out of the trunk that sunny morning, pleasantly warm and the air still fresh, as I lifted the cup to my mouth and took a sip of tea and watched Chris with his lazy overarm crawl swim up the pool to the steps. There he stopped and stood on the first step, turned and saw me sitting at the other end and dived back into the pool and swam to me.

"It's a great way to start the day man," he said, his elbows resting on the side of the pool, "Come on in."

I thought for a moment, not really relishing the thought of a sudden rush of cool water over my warm body.

"Come on you tart!" he said and splashed water over me.

That did it. I put down my teacup, stood and swiped off my Sloppy Joe top, stepped to the edge and dived in.

The uncomfortable rush of cool water was fleeting as an energising sensation took control of my muscles and I reached out with my strokes feeling a surge of power through my body.

"For Christ's sake, they're both at it now!" I heard Brett shout to Ed, "You'll have to do something about this, Sergeant Major."

That evening, a few minutes before 1900, the four of us arrived at Cactus and waved through the main gate. We continued up the drive to the inner gate and parked.

We were met by Gale in the president's front garden, "Hi guys, Merry Christmas," he said, as we noticed the motorcade lined up outside the house. "He's going to a party at his mother's house for the evening. You'll not be getting much down time tonight. Sorry guys, and you're on 'maximum standby' from now."

"Gale, I haven't brought any party clothes," said Ed scratching his head.

We all laughed and put our bags and day sacks into the chase vehicle parked behind the president's two vehicles and shrugged into our tac vests and stood-to on the steps by the entrance door.

"Deano, you drive mate," ordered Ed and Deano climbed into his vehicle and started the engine, revved it a couple of times, then satisfied, turned off the engine and remained seated at the steering wheel. There's nothing like being all lined-up waiting for the client, the client arriving and being driven off in their vehicle and leaving you behind because your vehicle would not start. Talk about egg on faces.

Still no sign of our counterparts though.

The door opened, and the president and first lady with Dancer and Prancer and his close friend and confident, Franc Joseph, stepped out of the house.

This is going to be a laugh, I thought, as Ed turned to greet them, and I turned outwards facing the front garden for any threats as Ed now escorted them to their vehicle. Then Deano called out in just above a whisper and with heavy sarcasm, "Here they come," and glancing to my left and seeing our counterparts sprinting to their vehicle, I could imagine what the first lady must be thinking.

I jumped in the back of our chase vehicle. Ed was waiting by the president's open rear vehicle door and the president climbed in as Chris, escorting the first lady and the children, opened her door and they all got in and sat next to him. Then, as the motorcade began to move, Ed and Chris quickly got into our chase vehicle, Ed up front next to Deano and Chris next to me. As the motorcade gathered speed, we opened the rear windows and brought our rifles up. Ed, in the front seat, opened his and stuck the Uzi out.

"There's something about Franc Joseph that makes me think of death," I ventured, and there were murmurs of agreement.

The motorcade had reached the main gate and would now turn sharply left on the road back towards the team house on Mountain Noir. Deano accelerated our vehicle to the president's right side to screen any threat from our right, then neatly dropping back behind again and covering the left.

"Nicely done Deano," said Ed, as the motorcade increased speed on the wide and empty road.

The house was only just short of a three ways crossroads and waiting steel rod and soon we turned off the road and up a track for a quarter of a mile and there was the president's mother's house, all lit up like a multi-coloured beacon, a sentinel giving light over the countryside, the house lights blazing in every room from top to bottom.

The doors opened and out spilled the president's mother surrounded by the rest of the family and close friends all shouting, "Joyous Noel." As the president's vehicle stopped, we bomb burst out from ours, almost before Deano had come to a stop and surrounded his vehicle.

The president's family in the doorway, now stood quiet in anticipation, waiting for the first family's appearance, as Franc Joseph alighted from the front, spoke briefly and I thought, urgently to Ed who was now standing by his door. Ed looked over at me on the other side of the vehicle and standing by the first lady's door, I briefly glanced at Chris who was standing a short distance away with his back to the house, rifle up and coving the garden, then turned and looked back over to Ed and nodded. Ed opened the president's door, allowing him to climb out, as I opened the first lady's door, allowing her and the children to get out.

None of us were happy about the lighting display, especially Franc Joseph. This Christmas night transfer of the president was not especially high on the risk scale, but any complacency and the watchers would take note for another time and place. It's all the small things that makes the big things work. The danger was constant, and every seemingly casual and apparently low risk move had to be thought through, risk assessed, and then managed.

Once again, our counterparts told us they had risk assessed everything earlier and given the location the all clear.

Yeah right!

The point being to remember is that in the president's armoured vehicle, they were safe up to a point. The risk was getting them from the vehicle into another reasonably safe place, the house in this instance. These drills become slick and rapid, especially when working with regular teams and for any watcher seeing this enbus or debus done properly gave them pause for thought and hopefully made them look for another target or another time.

I walked the first lady and the children round the back of the vehicle, and they joined the others at the door and stood hugging and kissing everyone as Ed and I looked at each other, willing this formality to end. The whole family were now silhouetted in the frame of the doors and looking over at Deano, still sat behind the wheel of our chase vehicle, should there be the need to evacuate everyone rapidly, I smiled my agreement as he rolled his eyes at the scene on the front porch.

Bloody get inside you lot! I shouted silently in my head and saw Franc Joseph who was speaking to Ed, notice the danger and began ushering them quickly inside the house.

"We'll leave the motorcade here," said Ed and walked off, pointing to where he wanted the guards to be posted as Deano, Chris and I found a garden bench just a few feet from our chase vehicle and settled down.

Ed returned and took the cup of coffee I offered and said, "Franc said its Christmas and to relax. Nothing's going to happen tonight. They're all in church praying, so no worries."

Yeah right! I thought, When I'm told not to worry is when I start worrying," and stood up saying, "I'm going to do a recce and see if there's another way out of this place.

"Good idea mate," Ed replied.

"I'll come with you. You brought any chocolate?" said Chris.

It had been a long Christmas night and the four of us were tired by the time the day team arrived. Ed gave the handover to Brett who roundly and amusingly abused us all for being able to go back to our team house and chill.

So, with Brett's, "And don't be late tonight!" still in our ears, we drove off laughing.

At the team house, I remember I was too tired to eat breakfast and so said my goodnight to my friends and went to my room.

On reaching the door I looked for the spider. It was not there!

Oh Christ. The evil thing's in my room!"

.

Chapter 12

My Unquiet Heart

I have always been restless. As a young lad at school, I believe I read too many adventure books, gripping yarns, as they were known. Later, as a young man, these books had left me wanting to travel, seek adventure, and I did. Travelling overland to the very tip of India, first having been arrested in Jerusalem at the border point going into Israel, at a time when the only entrance from the Arab Middle East was the Mendelbaum Gate. One of the two travelling companions who had attached themselves to my friend and I, was found to have hashish on him, and so we were all taken off to prison. This delicate young man was German and kept insisting, "We are guests in your country!" Only he would pronounce guest as 'chest.' He was soon told to shut up in old fashioned Anglo Saxon, he understood that.

A few days later, young Rudolph, this gentle, sensitive lad, was fined, and we were released, having been well treated throughout our stay. There was one incident that left me amused though. During our stay at the Citadel, Jerusalem's prison, Rudolph was visited by the German consul, a fine, tall, straight-backed gentleman, clearly from the German officer class, with what I took to be a sabre scar on his left cheek. He greeted us formally inquiring about our welfare, and so young Rudolph, this dear sensitive soul, took the opportunity to complain that he was made to sleep on the floor, and it was uncomfortable for his back. The consul drew himself up, rigid-backed to attention and barked, "It is good for your posture!" He then turned and exited the room. Poor Rudolph broke down in tears; I could not keep a straight face. Strangely though, the Palestinian police officer in charge of the prison, a tough brute of a man, showed Rudolph unexpected sympathy, kindly giving him another filthy, grease- encrusted blanket to lie on, saying in broken English, "You are a guest in my country."

Not 'chest.'

Then flying from India to Thailand, Burma was a closed country then, and all the way down the peninsular to Singapore and onward to Australia. I had other adventures on the way and in that wonderful land of Australia. When I finally returned to the UK, some two years or so later, I found that my life here was just not big enough to hold my interest, and so I continued to look for the thrill, now known to me as the buzz!

But it was a curse.

Over the years, the curse, has taken me to the very edge of life, where I have tasted the poisonous allure of mortal danger, taken me into battle, with weapons and more often without, just hands and anything I could lay my hands on. I say this without any sense of boasting, just what needed to be done at that moment in time, either in defence of myself and or others, or just getting the job done, and take no pride in the curse. But now, towards the end of my physical capability, I still wait for the call from certain friends saying, *"We need you here asap!"* Music to my ears, and so I would still rush to the nearest airport and jump on a flight to wherever, that very afternoon.

I had a call from Ed recently saying something was cooking in a South American country I had never been to before. Ooh Aah! I checked my grab bag and passport and pointed my desert boots towards the door, wondering how I would get it past my wife and family first.

Barre Foster had wanted me in Bristol and there also was the lovely girl I had met years previously and stayed in touch with. We were married a year later.

Barre had been having problems with the Bath racecourse gang who were making themselves unpleasant in the night club. I introduced myself to them over the next few weeks and more than gave the good news to their frontman, Snowy and received a bollocking from a pissed off CID officer who said Snowy was his snitch and to please leave him alone. Oddly enough, that crowd of idiots never came to the night club again. It must have been something I said.

Some years earlier, Barre had contacted me saying Phil Tate needed to speak to me. Phil was then running the Mecca theatrical agency and said he wanted me to look after Dusty Springfield for a few days, as she was on a promotional tour of several Mecca ballrooms in London, plugging her latest record.

I was young, stupid, big and good looking and was convinced this international singing star would probably be unable to resist me.

We were together for about four evenings, as I recall. She very nice and polite to me but appeared to show no attraction to me. My thoughts were, *She must be mad,* as I tried to understand and make sense of her irrational behaviour. So, following this tour and her saying nice words to Phil about how professional I was, there was not a mention of how much she must have fancied me.

And so dear reader, I lived with this rejection for something like twenty-five years before I was told by a pal that Dusty Springfield was gay!

"Gay! Are you sure?" I demanded.

Apparently, it was common knowledge in showbiz circles, but Phil Tate had not told me!

Well! That put a smile on my face. For twenty-five years I had lived in the false knowledge I had been rejected by this lovely lady. But no, it was not me, of course not. I felt so relieved that my failure was nothing to do with me.

Silly boy!

I came to love the West Country and all points south, and for a few years, while the children were young, moved to the countryside some miles south of Bristol. Sadly though, we found that the country folk were tight lipped and would look at us and our children as if we had recently arrived from another world. At the bottom of our lane was a small Co-op supermarket. There, the manageress, small, round and middle aged, would watch us with suspicious eyes and hide the daily bread delivery under the counter to save it for her regulars and friends. Whenever my wife or I would ask for bread, we were told it had sold out. It was not long, of course, before I had had enough of this bull and told her to "give me a loaf of the bloody bread, it's under your bloody counter!" That was the end of any further shopping in that friendly corner shop.

A lovely place to live, but most locals, whose families had lived there for generations, were insular and unwelcoming. It really did not bother me, but it upset my wife and my older daughter was bullied at the local college. There was the time when we had a visit from the local country hard man complaining about something or other, I never did find out what. His only problem was he had not realised until it was too late, he had taken a tiger by the tale and the tiger turned on him.

I had to work late-nights and an early morning drive back home was getting too much. So, we moved back to Bristol, partly because of the drive, but also for work opportunities for our older daughter, and a better school for the youngest.

On starting my own business, I was to meet a rainbow of others, who would use and pay for my managerial talents. For example, there was Joe, a nice man, originally from Sicily who was a professional gambler and a successful restaurateur. I would look after his restaurant on the weekend evenings, as it was on the route home from Bristol town centre to a tough housing estate for all the yobs who had just painted the town red, and when Joe went gambling, I would again look after him as it would become very fractious and volatile after a few hours round the poker table. I was there to keep Joe out of trouble, even though he started most of it.

My unquiet heart had taken me a long way from home and the family. I was earning excellent money which my wife would later use to buy us a lovely apartment on the beautiful Greek island of Kefalonia. She had holidayed there with our daughters and their families and had fallen in love with the place. I was working somewhere or other, so had not been home for months, but every evening, my shift pattern, the weather, and the atmospherics permitting, we would talk on Skype or mobile phone. And so, one evening, she informed me that she was buying an apartment there. Of course, I had never seen the skies over Kefalonia and had to look at the atlas to see where this island was in Greece.

As usual, my wife had it just right, as one evening, I met her at Athens airport, and we caught the short flight to the island. We would spend many a month holidaying there with our family, and from Athens airport, I could fly to anywhere I happened to be working at the time.

I would think of my family and their lives and our futures when sat in the dark under the mango tree outside the president's and first lady's kitchen door at their forty-acre plantation. He knew when I was on night duty and in the quiet of the night, I would sit there, rifle across my knees. On one occasion, I heard him telling a servant to switch off the kitchen light and so keep me in the dark and hidden in the deep shadow of the tree, unseen even from a few feet away.

Fully grown mango trees are huge, and when the mango fruit is ripe it will just drop from the tree and come smashing through the foliage and hit the ground like a bomb. If struck on the head, it would be the end of you, killed by flying fruit!

It was after one such night duty, we were told there had been a mutiny in the prison outside the town of Gonaeve on the northern claw. Most of the guards had been slaughtered and there were reports that some had been eaten. The mutineers were calling themselves the cannibal army (that title alone was enough to send shivers down our spines), and they were threatening the town. Our small unit immediately cleaned our weapons, sourced extra ammunition, packed our daysacks with MREs (Meals Ready-to-Eat) and water, and stood-to, waiting for what we all knew was coming.

It came the following morning. Gale issued the order. The entire detail of the presidential protection unit would muster and escort the president to Gonaeve, where he would address the town's folk at the football stadium, next to the town's main square, then take mass in the cathedral. He would also visit a school to reassure the children. This would mean those of us who were on the security advance party again, would have to split our small unit to have advance cover at the school, at the stadium and at the cathedral. Luckily, this time we would have more manpower to juggle with.

Chris Gibson would secure and wait at the school and Chris, Ed and myself would advance on to the square and stadium. Please do not think Wembley for the stadiums in Haiti, they were much smaller affairs with just four or five rows of concrete terracing. However, shortly before we were due to leave, orders were changed as they so often are and Gibby would now travel with some of our counterparts to the school, and the three of us would travel with the motorcade, increasing its firepower should it come under attack. Our American comrades loved firepower!

I felt uncomfortable about Gibby, to all intents and purposes, being alone at the school, knowing should his position go 'hot', our counterparts would take to their heels. I had spoken with Gale, suggesting I would support Gibby. Gale shook his head and said I was needed at the stadium. Smiling, he added that he wished he had more men. And so, mid-morning, we drove in motorcade to Gonaeve. The journey there was uneventful and on coming to the school, we drove past without stopping and I caught a glance of a smiling Gibby, standing alone, without any sign of our counterparts but surrounded by laughing school children. Franc Joseph had decided to miss out the president's visit to the school, as he did not want the drive back to Port au Prince to be in the dark. Again, there was that Haitian thing about the darkness. Chris Gibson would later meet with us at the stadium. The three of us admired Gibby for his part in the day's mission. He had been very exposed and in very real danger if any elements of the cannibal army were hungry and had decided to eat him.

It must be said though, there were and are, those that would quietly take themselves out of the line of fire, and I recall a day in Port au Prince, screening the president from possible danger when one of our number almost unnoticed, stepped from our screen and took cover at the safe side of the building. What surprised me though, it was the man I would up to then, have been happy to walk through the gates of hell beside. It left me saddened and confused that a man with his background had done this.

But then again, dear reader, the collective roar of some hundreds of hostile people making it obvious that they wanted blood, would be overwhelming and unmanageable for some. Therefore, I do not judge. I was just saddened, as I well remember the time that I first experienced something like this, when the noise alone almost knocked me off my feet, never mind the associated blood curdling threats.

And so, the curse goes on.

But you know, it's the little things in life that probably nobody else would notice that hold all the big things together for me.

The nice thing about the Haiti contract was that I was paid while on leave, an unusual situation but one reflecting the threat level there. Also, we could be recalled anytime during our leave.

I was on my return from Haiti after a long, sweaty, twelve weeks. I was on a month's leave. I had managed to get a flight from Miami to Amsterdam or perhaps it was Paris and from there, I was able to get a flight into Bristol. Usually, I would find myself having to fly into Heathrow and from there, have to get myself home to Bristol.

Coming through customs and there waiting for me, was my wife, our two daughters, their husbands and my three grandsons.

Ooh Aah!

The unexpected sight of my family was overwhelming. I gritted my teeth and swallowed down the lump in my throat, as my two eldest grandsons ran to me, hugged me and kissed me. The youngest, just a toddler the last time I had seen him, walked shyly up to me, held out his arms for me to pick him up, then wrapped those arms round my neck and kissed me.

I quickly blinked away my tears, as I was surrounded by the rest of my family. It was a wonderful private moment. One of the little things.

Looking forward to spending the next month with my family, we left the airport and went to my youngest daughter's home for a celebration dinner with me looking forward so much, to reconnecting with everyone I loved. But I knew towards the end of my leave, the curse would return and have a word with my unquiet heart, and I would find myself masking the fact that I was looking forward to getting back and feeling the buzz again.

And so now, Ed, Chris and I are waiting for the next job to be offered. It's been sometime since we have worked together, the waiting appears to be getting longer and longer, with me missing the buzz dreadfully. Mind you, we are all knocking on a bit, but I still have the feelings I had as a schoolboy. Gerry agrees, adding I behave like one frequently.

Silly old fool!

So currently, I drive an ambulance with a dedicated team of clinicians, usually a paediatric consultant, a senior advanced nurse practitioner and senior staff nurses, recovering dangerously sick and injured children from hospitals throughout the region and taking them to Centres of Excellence here in Bristol and elsewhere, sometimes blue lighting these children to Great Ormond Street (GOS) for life saving operations.

And so, late on a Sunday afternoon, the call came in to scramble to Bristol Children's to take a very dangerously ill baby, just a few weeks old to GOS for an urgent operation that dare not be delayed.

Late afternoon meant that the medical team and me would be hours late finishing. None of us looked forward to that.

The baby was collected by the team from the paediatric ITU and hooked-up to the monitors, syringe pumps and respirators on our stretcher, a process that most times, can take well over an hour, usually nearly two. Finally, baby loaded onto the ambulance, mum sat in the front seat next to me, all the medics in the back with baby, watching the monitors. I had been told by the senior clinician that baby desperately needed this operation, but it was a very dangerous one, and he did not expect a good outcome. The mood in the back was solemn, everyone with eyes on the monitors. Mum was quiet, in her own world of dread.

The consultant said simply, "Get us there as quickly as possible. The surgeon is waiting in theatre!"

I drove on 'Blues' (blue lights) rapidly along the M4 and into London where, for some reason, my satnav decided to stop working. Mum volunteered to guide me to GOS using her phone and the exchanges between us became humorous and amused us both. It took mum out of herself for those few minutes and we both connected.

It's mentally draining driving that distance on 'Blues', especially through London traffic, and on arrival at GOS, the team and I quickly unloaded baby and rushed through the corridors finally arriving at

Children's ITU where a team of medics were waiting. They swooped on baby to prepare the child for the surgical team.

Our job had finished, with baby and mum safely delivered to one of the world's centres of excellence for sick children. I looked over the medical team I was with, James the consultant, Colin, the acute nurse practitioner and Ali, the senior staff nurse. They all looked exhausted after two and a half hours in the back of a speeding, rolling ambulance with constant three tone sirens screaming in their ears, total focus on the baby, the monitors, the syringes and the respirator. They were shattered, so was I and I still had to drive back to Bristol. But you know, we all had a sense of having done something worthwhile that evening, hopefully, all being a part of that baby's slender chance of survival and mum's well-being.

I asked Colin how the baby was during the journey, he looked me in the eyes, raised his eyebrows and said, "It's a dangerous operation baby has to go through…".

"Oh dear," I thought, another bad memory to stuff into my overloaded bad memory cupboard and try to get that door closed.

The following Sunday was my birthday and again, I was working on babies, when the call from the medics upstairs was, "Martyn, we have a repat' from GOS back to Children's."

"*What!*" I thought, "*Not another trip to London. Bloody hell, I only did that last Sunday. And it's my birthday.*"

"Leaving in ten minutes," they added.

"*Ten minutes! It's my birthday!*"

The whole team arrived, and we took a nice relaxed drive to GOS. The medics were relaxed and chatting, no pressure this trip. We were all unaware we were collecting the baby we had taken to GOS the previous Sunday. Besides, it was a different medical team.

On arrival on the ward, I immediately recognised mum who came up to me saying baby's operation had been successful and baby was going to be alright. She introduced me to dad who took my hand and told me how grateful everyone in their family were.

It was wonderful news I had not expected; indeed, I had stuffed the memory of the previous Sunday away in a cupboard somewhere deep in my mind. I remembered it was also my birthday and it dawned on me what a wonderful gift I had been given.

I had played just a minor part in this child's chances of survival and it had a happy ending.

It was the best birthday present I have ever had, and I felt so good.

Hurrah!

Epilogue

That Bloody Spider

I was sitting in one of our poolside chairs by the house end of the pool at our team house on Mountain Noir reading under a tropical hardwood. The hardwood played host to what, at the time, I took to be a parasite orchid. I have since learnt that orchids are mainly epiphytes which grow on other plants, particularly trees. This orchid was one of the most beautifully delicate, exotically colourful orchids I had ever seen and to add to this serene beauty were hummingbirds that would visit this flower, as I reclined comfortably just a few feet away.

I heard two rifle fire gunshots, but it was some distance away, followed by two harsh cracks above my head and an immediate change of air pressure with a sudden vibrating and disturbing rush-of-air sensation.

Someone had taken a couple of shots at me. I must have been visible from the road in our swimming pool seating area, giving us wonderful and now potentially fatal views of Mountain Noir. Someone had taken the opportunity to try and bag a Blanc.

This opportunistic attempt on my life really pissed me off and I jumped up from the pool lounger and ran to the low wall overlooking the road to see if I could get sight of the shooter.

Angry and now amusingly reckless, I jumped up and down, waving my arms above my head shouting, "It's my fucking day off, you tosser!"

I could not see anyone, the shooter either hiding in the undergrowth or having driven off.

"Who are you shouting at?" It was Chris looking over his balcony at me, puzzled.

"Someone's just taken a couple of pot shots at me," I replied indignantly. Gun fire was common and unless you were being fired at, or on task with the president, normally we would not take much notice.

"I wouldn't sit there then," Chris said, laughing at my antics.

"I like it here!" I replied, petulantly and picked up my book, stepped back to my recliner, lowered the back down a few notches, reached out and pulled my duty belt and pistol closer and continued reading, but thoughts reminding me of the continuous presence of danger lurking in this wonderful island paradise.

Had the shooter been more accurate or the weapon scoped......then the realisation dawned, "They know where we live!"

Chris appeared beside me saying, "Ed's waiting for us at the Fiore de Latte, let's get some lunch."

"Okay." *It's probably safer there.* I thought.

Another time .... It was a black tropical night, no moon, heavy, dark, foreboding cloud cover, with the distant rumble of thunder warning of an approaching storm.

I was sat in a comfortable patio chair under my mango tree just a few feet from the president's kitchen door, just over my left shoulder. The light was off in the kitchen and my side of the house was in darkness. The night was now silent as if nature was holding its breath, bracing herself and waiting for the threatening storm.

I sat, rifle over my knees as usual, tactically positioned so I had only to drop my left hand to find the rifle's pistol grip and then to bring it to the ready at my left shoulder.

At night, in the dark, speed and the silence when bringing up the weapon to the ready, would or could, make a difference.

My head and shoulders were wrapped with an olive coloured towel, shemagh fashion, keeping the mosquitoes from my face, head and neck and more importantly, my short white hair and face that would have stood out like a lighthouse beam in the darkness.

The thunder was getting closer, lightening momentarily illuminating the sky above, throwing trees and other foliage to suddenly appear naked and menacing. This was mother nature at her most dramatic and nothing else, I reminded myself, but this was Haiti, and perhaps Baron Samadi would prowl the stormy night.

"Some tough guy, Jones," I told myself.

And so, I took the rifle from my knees and tucked the butt under my left elbow, seeking its comfort and reassurance.

I was suddenly startled, for without warning, a torrent of heavy tropical rain swept into my position of comfort under the mango tree and I needed to change position, find somewhere dry and safe to wait out the storm. I ran across the patio, past the French windows, where, on light summer evenings, I would sit and listen to President Aristide playing classical music wonderfully on his grand piano, to the archway separating the private rear gardens from the front of house and more formal front gardens. I stopped, hoping the archway would give me some protection from the torrential, pounding rain. Each time the lightening flashed, it displayed hundreds of huge raindrop strikes on the patio, followed by foot high plumes of splashes that seemed to dance rhythmically across the patio and the asphalt of the drive, and I was getting wetter and wetter.

Just feet from the archway was a bin store, the entrance masked by bushes and unseen from the rear garden. It was a dry place for me to shelter, but I hesitated. The bin store I knew, was full of cobwebs and where there's cobwebs, there's spiders!

Oh, I dreaded those bloody things, they gave me the creeps.

However, my trousers were now soaking wet and the water was beginning to fill my boots and of course, starting to work its wet way up towards the crutch of my trousers and I was starting to feel cold down there.

No choice, I ran the few feet towards the entrance of the bin store, brushing past the dripping wet bushes adding to my sopping misery, stopped and checked the doorway for cobwebs using my torch. I know, I know, what on earth was I doing using a torch while on guard duty, possibly giving away my position to a watcher?

I know, I know! But I was terrified alright…of the bloody spiders that were waiting for me in there. So, quickly brushing away cobwebs around and anywhere near the doorway, I stood post among the obscene stuff of nightmares until the rainstorm passed, my concentration focused more on any movement behind me, in the store than any bad guys creeping through the gardens towards the house.

As the rain began to fade away and keeping to deep shadow, I moved slowly and quietly back to my favoured position under the mango tree. The seat was wet, so brushing off surface water, I sat down. I was wet anyway, so a bit more wet would not make any difference to my discomfort. Anyway, I would be dried out by first light.

I loved nights at Cactus and sat hidden in the rest of the darkness, enjoying the light show of lightening and the grumble of thunder, as it faded away in the distance.

And so dear reader, I have one last confession before ending my personal narrative of my time in that strangely wonderful, disturbingly mysterious isle of Haiti, and that is why I think, I shot that fucking spider that lived outside my room door.

It was late, it was dark. I was tired, sweaty, dusty and dirty, as I made my way to my room following a long day. Reaching my door, I looked at the entrance hole of the spider's lair.

It was not there. Why, was it in my room?

I opened the door and stepped inside and reaching out for the light switch flicked it on. The overhead light was dull and glowed just enough for me to see into the corners. Of course, I saw nothing. But I knew that things between me and the spider had come to a head.

It had tipped me over the edge!

Dropping my day sack and stashing my rifle, I drew my Glock from its holster, stepped back to my room door, opened it and fired two nine millimetre rounds down the spider's hole.

Ed opened his door, "What's going on?"

"Just saying goodbye to that fucking spider."

Ed grinned, "Get to bed mate."

I stepped into the bathroom, stripped off my clothing, turned on the shower and checked the spider was not lurking anywhere in the shower, washed and stepped out of the shower and reached for my towel, flicking it out first to make sure the spider was not hiding in any of the folds. Gathering my dirty clothing, I opened my door and dropped the clothing outside for the ladies to wash and iron in the morning; I intended to have a couple of hours lie in. I glanced at the spider's now smashed entrance hole, no sign of the thing, stepped back inside my room and pulled back the sheeting on my bed to see if the spider was lurking in the bedclothes. No sign of the thing. Finally, before getting into bed, I placed the Glock under my pillow, radio on my bedside table and looked under the bed before climbing in. Still no sign of the thing.

I turned off the light and slept for hours.

Any other questions you may have dear reader must of course remain unanswered.